Integrated English

TRANSITIONS

1

STUDENT BOOK

Linda Lee

Oxford University Press

Oxford University Press
198 Madison Avenue
New York, NY 10016 USA

Great Clarendon Street
Oxford OX2 6DP England

Oxford New York
Auckland Bangkok Buenos Aires Cape Town Chennai
Dar es Salaam Delhi Hong Kong Istanbul Karachi
Kolkata Kuala Lumpur Madrid Melbourne Mexico City
Mumbai Nairobi São Paulo Shanghai Singapore Taipei
Tokyo Toronto

with an associated company in Berlin

OXFORD is a trademark of Oxford University Press.

Copyright © 1998 Oxford University Press

Library of Congress Cataloging-In-Publication Data

Lee, Linda, 1950–
  Transitions 1: student book / Linda Lee.
  p. cm. — (Integrated English)
  ISBN 0-19-434622-6
  1. English language—Textbooks for foreign speakers. I. Title.
II. Series.
PE1128.L43   1998
428.2'4 — dc21   97-9680

Senior Editor: Jeff Krum
Production Editor: Tyrone Prescod

Design Project Manager: Mark C. Kellogg
Design/Production Assistants: David Easter,
  David Hildebrand, Brett Sonnenschein
Art Buyers: Donna Goldberg, Nina Hess
Picture Researcher: Clare Maxwell
Production Manager: Abram Hall

Printing (last digit): 10 9 8
Printed in China

Cover direction: Shelley Himmelstein
Cover design/photo montage: R. S. Winter

Illustrations by: Mike Hertz Associates, John Holder, Candace
Lourdes, Steve Sandford, Jean & Mou-Sien Tseng

Handwriting and realia by: Todd Cooper/designlab; Claudia
Kehrhahn; Scott A. MacNeil/MacNeil & MacIntosh; Karen
Minot; Rob Schuster; Nina Wallace

Location and studio photography by: Robert Holmes, Dennis
Kitchen, Monica Stevenson, Ken Tannenbaum, Stephen Ogilvy

**The publishers would like to thank the following for their
permission to reproduce photographs:** Barbara Alper/Stock
Boston; David Appleby/Photofest; Archive Photos; Joseph H.
Bailey/National Geographic Society; Tyler Beard/True West;
Marc & Evelyn Bernheim/Woodfin Camp; Elihu Blotnick/
Woodfin Camp; Marus Boesch/Allsport; David Boynton/Photo
Resource Hawaii; Bridegman Art Library, by Courtesy of the
Trustees of the Victoria & Albert Museum; John Callahan/Tony
Stone Images; Wendy Chan/The Image Bank; Aaron Chang;
Dann Coffey/Comstock; Corbis/Bettmann Archive; Culver
Pictures; Bob Daemmrich/Stock Boston; Tami Dawson/Photo
Resource Hawaii; John Eascott/Yva Momatiuk/DRK Photo; John
Elk/Stock Boston; Everett Collection; ExpressNewspapers/
Archive Photos; Werner Forman/Art Resource, NY; Tracy
Frankel; Tony Freeman/Photo Edit; Robert Frerck/Woodfin
Camp; Twice Gibson/Pacific Stock; Porter Gifford/Liaison
International; Lou Goldman/New Line Cinema/Photofest;
Simon Grosset/Liaison International; David W. Hamilton/The
Image Bank; Ray Hand; Robert Harding Picture Library; Dale
Higgins/Liaison International; Henry Horenstein; Julie
Houck/Stock Boston; Richard Hume Photography; Jeff
Hunter/The Image Bank; Marcel Isy-Schwart/The Image Bank;
Jacana/Photo Researchers, Inc.; Reed Kaestner/Viesti Associates;
Catherine Karnow/Woodfin Camp; Ron Kimball Photography;
Don Klumpp/The Image Bank; David Leah/Allsport; Erich
Lessing/Art Resource, NY; Story Litchfield/Stock Boston; R. Ian
Lloyd/The Stock Market; David Lokey/Jack Affleck/Vail
Associates; Dr. Kari Lounatmaa/SPL/Photo Researchers, Inc.;
Elliot Marks/Paramount Pictures/The Kobal Collection; Ned
Matura/Liaison International; Walter McBride/Retna; Fred
McConnaughey/Photo Researchers, Inc.; Amanda Merulla/
Stock Boston; Metropolitan Museum of Art, purchase 1934,
34.22.1; MGM/The Kobal Collection; Hank Morgan/Photo
Researchers, Inc.; Tony Mottram/Retna; The Natural History
Museum, London; Lance Nelson/The Stock Market; The
Newark Museum/Art Resource, NY; Joseph Nicephore Niepce/
Harry Ransom Humanities Research Center, Univ. of Texas at
Austin; Michael Nichols/Magnum Photos; John K. Ogata/Photo
Resource Hawaii; Jim Olive/Tony Stone Images; Paramount
Pictures/Everett Collection; Richard Paisley/Stock Boston;
Richard Paisley/Viesti Associates; Robert Pearcy/Animals
Animals/Earth Scenes; Douglas Peebles Photography; Joe
Polillio/Liaison International; Dennis Purse/Photo Researchers,
Inc.; Richard Rinaldi/Impact Visuals; Marc Romanelli/The
Image Bank; Guido Rossi/The Image Bank; Franco Salmoiraghi/
Photo Resource Hawaii; S.B. Photography/Tony Stone Images;
Ben Simmons/The Stock Market; Czarek Sokolowski/AP
Photos; J.L. Stage/The Image Bank; Gret Stott/Masterfile; Keren
Su/Tony Stone Images; James Sugar/Black Star; Joseph
Szkodzinsky/The Image Bank; Craig Tuttle/The Stock Market;
Twentieth Century Fox/Photofest; Universal/International/The
Kobal Collection; Universal Pictures/The Kobal Collection;
UPI/Corbis/Bettmann Archive; Gerard Vandystadt/Allsport;
Richard Vogel/Liaison International; Frank Whitney/The Image
Bank

*The publishers would also like to thank the following for their
help:* Daytona Beach Area Convention & Visitor's Bureau;
Florida Keys TDC; Mac Media/Vail-Beaver Creek Magazine;
McDonald's; The MZTV Museum; Random House; Tom
Sanders/Trans-Atlantic Entertainment; Smith & Hawken; St.
Martin's Press

p. 4   David Ball/"The Stock Market, © Disney Enterprises, Inc."
p. 13 *Do's and Taboos Around the World*, by Roger E. Axtel.
Copyright © 1993. Reprinted by permission of John Wiley &
Sons, Inc.
p. 24 Photo courtesy of Harrison Carloss/Doc Martens USA.
p. 25 Photo by Patrick Demarchelier, Courtesy of British
Vogue, © Conde Naste Publishing.
p. 31 From *Are You Normal?* Copyright © 1995, by Bernice
Kanner. Reprinted by permission of St. Martin's Press Paperbacks.
p. 41 The following article is reprinted courtesy of *Sports
Illustrated for Kids* from the July 1995 issue. Copyright © 1995,
Time Inc. "Stars: Gabrielle Reece," by John Rolfe. All rights
reserved.
p. 45 The following article is reprinted courtesy of *Sports
Illustrated for Kids* from the March 1994 issue. Copyright ©
1994, Time Inc. "Stars: Mark Allen," by Pohla Smith. All rights
reserved.
p. 51 From *The Practical Guide to Practically Everything,* by
Peter Bernstein and Christopher Ma, editors. Copyright ©
1995, by Almanac, Inc. Reprinted by permission of Random
House, Inc.
p. 53 Photo by Wolfgang Dietze, painting by Carmen Lomas
Garza.
p. 56 From *Korean Folk and Fairy Tales,* by Suzanne Crowder
Han, Hollym Corporation, Publishers. Copyright © 1991, by
Suzanne Crowder Han.
p. 67 Photo courtesy of Maxell.
p. 71 Reprinted by permission of Farrar, Straus & Giroux, Inc.:
Excerpt from *How To,* by Peter Passell. Copyright © 1976, by
Peter Passell.

ACKNOWLEDGMENTS

The author and publisher would like to thank the following people for reviewing *Transitions*. Their comments and suggestions contributed to its development and helped shape its content.

Miguel Ivan Abreu, Instituto Tecnológico de Veracruz, Veracruz, Mexico

Ana Alaminos, Esc. Nal. Preparatoria No. 5-UNAM, Mexico City, Mexico

Timothy Allan, St. Mary's College, Nagoya, Japan

Charles Anderson, Athénée Français, Tokyo, Japan

Daniel Altamirano, CENLEX-IPN, Mexico City, Mexico

Kevin Bandy, Boston English Learners, Caracas, Venezuela

Barbara Bangle, CELE-UAEM, Toluca, Mexico

Eleanor Kirby Barnes, Athénée Français, Tokyo, Japan

Diane Burnett, Tokyo Women's Christian University, Tokyo, Japan

Paul Cameron, International Trade Institute, Hsinchu, Taiwan

Kyung-Whan Cha, Chung Ang University, Seoul, Korea

Katie Chiba, Trident School of Languages, Nagoya, Japan

Steve Cornwell, Osaka Jogakuin Junior College, Osaka, Japan

Lynn Napoli Costa, ICBEU, Belo Horizonte, Brazil

Katy Cox, Casa Thomas Jefferson, Brasília, Brazil

Lucia de Aragão, União Cultural, São Paulo, Brazil

Marion DeLarche, Kanda University of International Studies, Chiba, Japan

Jacob de Ruiter, CELE-UAEM, Toluca, Mexico

Montserrat Muntaner Djmal, IBEU, Rio de Janeiro, Brazil

Jasna Dubravcic, Showa Women's University, Tokyo, Japan

Rosa Erlichman, Unãio Cultural, São Paulo, Brazil

Alejandra Gallegos, Interlingua, Aguascalientes, Ags., Mexico

Ismael Garrido, CELE-Benemérita Universidad Autónoma de Puebla, Puebla, Mexico

Christine Gascho, Bunka Institute of Language, Tokyo, Japan

Peter Gobel, Ritsumeikan University, Kyoto, Japan

Noni Goertzen, Aichi Shukutoku Junior College, Nagoya, Japan

Ann-Marie Hadzima, National Taiwan University, Taipei, Taiwan

Pamela Hu, Taiwan Boys High School, Tainan, Taiwan

Diana Jones, Grupo Educativo Angloamericano, S.C., Mexico City, Mexico

Atsuko Kashiwagi, Showa Women's University, Tokyo, Japan

Mia Kim, Kyung-Hee University, Seoul, Korea

Nick Lambert, Toyo University, Tokyo, Japan

Jean-Pierre Louvrier, IBEU-CE, Fortaleza, Brazil

Angus Macindoe, Aichi University, Miyoshi, Japan

Gabriela Martínez, CEMARC, Mexico City, Mexico

Bruce McAlpine, University of Toronto, Toronto, Canada

Anne Newell McDonald, Hajiyama University, Hiroshima, Japan

Jane McElroy, Aoyama Gakuin University, Tokyo, Japan

Elías Mennhar, Vizcainas School, Mexico City, Mexico

Joaquín Meza, Esc. Nal. Preparatoria No. 7-UNAM, Mexico City, Mexico

Joann Miller, Universidad del Valle, Mexico City, Mexico

Rick Nelson, Matsuyama University, Evergreen Language School, Matsuyama, Japan

Mary Sisk Noguchi, Meijo University Junior College, Nagoya, Japan

Terry O'Brien, Otani Women's University, Osaka, Japan

Sonia Ocampo, Bertha von Glumer School, Mexico City, Mexico

Gary Ockey, Kanda University of International Studies, Chiba, Japan

Mary Oliveira, IBEU, Rio de Janeiro, Brazil

Cynthia Omoto, Kagoshima Junshin University, Sendai, Japan

Aída Orozco, Esc. Nal. Preparatoria No. 5-UNAM, Mexico City, Mexico

Dawn Paullin, Asia University, Tokyo, Japan

John Perkins, Tokyo Foreign Language College, Tokyo, Japan

Lara Perry, Time-Life English Language School, Yonago, Japan

Augustine Paul Porter, Grupo Educativo Angloamericano S.C., Mexico City, Mexico

César Regnier, CELE-Benemérita Universidad Autónoma de Puebla, Puebla, Mexico

Yolanda Reyes, Esc. Nal. Preparatoria No. 6-UNAM, Mexico City, Mexico

Carol Rinnert, Hiroshima City University, Hiroshima, Japan

Peggy Rule, St. Mary's College, Nagoya, Japan

Marie Adele Ryan, Associacão Alumni, São Paulo, Brazil

Jennifer Sakano, Keio Shonan Fujisawa High School, Fujisawa, Japan

Silvia Sandoval, Instituto Mexicano del Petroleo, Mexico City, Mexico

Debora Schisler, Seven Language School, São Paulo, Brazil

Gregory Strong, Aoyama Gakuin University, Tokyo, Japan

Tamara Swenson, Osaka Jogakuin Junior College, Osaka, Japan

Oscar Vásquez, Universidad del Valle, Mexico City, Mexico

Catherine Vellinga, University of Toronto, Toronto, Canada

Patricia Verduzco, CELEX-IPN, Mexico City, Mexico

M. Angel Vidagna, CECYT, Mexico City, Mexico

Roberto Viera, CAFAM, Bogotá, Colombia

Adele Villela, Universidad Latinoamericana, Mexico City, Mexico

Fu-Hsang Wang, Nan Tai College, Tainan, Taiwan

Julian Woolhouse, Japan College of Foreign Languages, Tokyo

The publisher and author would like to thank the following people for contributing ideas, personal stories, and cultural information for use in *Transitions*: Sue Brioux Aldcorn, Amanda Block, Simon Byrne, Aaron Chang, Octavio Diaz, Irene Frankel, Roger Garcia, Kamal Gürer, Victoria Kimbrough, Dorsey Kleitz, Yi Liu, Sandi Lucore, Bill and Sue Mattison, Greg Sergi, Noi Suwannik, Yoko Tezuka, and Sylvia Wheeldon.

The author would also like to thank the following people at OUP who offered many helpful insights and suggestions: Karen Brock, Bev Curran, Silvia Dones de Sauza, Chris Foley, Roy Gilbert, Robert Habbick, Todashi Kambara, Steve Maginn, Toshiki Matsuda, and Paul Riley.

Scope and Sequence

Listening	Reading	Process Writing (Workbook)
• Listening for specific times of day • Listening for details about someone's trip	• "A Day in the Life of an MTV Intern" • "Five Days in Florida" • "Vacation Questionnaire" (WB)	Writing a questionnaire • Brainstorming • Proofreading
• Identifying how people describe their likes and dislikes • Collecting information on people's jobs	• "Life on Top of a Mountain" • "Would You Like to Have This Job?" • "Low Pay and Free Food" (WB)	Writing a summary • Summarizing • Collecting information
• Comparing customs in different countries • Listening for information to confirm your predictions	• "Do's and Taboos Around the World" • "How Do You Greet People?" • "Men, Women, and Body Language" (WB)	Expressing an Opinion • Giving examples • Collecting ideas
• Listening for specific information about clothing • Listening for people's opinions on clothing	• "Three Outfits from the 1700s" • "Footwear Fads" • "Down with Neckties!" (WB)	Expressing an opinion • Analyzing a paragraph • Listing ideas
• Determining if speakers agree or disagree • Listening for details about people's habits	• "The Story of Jim Lewis and Jim Springer" • "Are You Normal?" • "TV Behavior" (WB)	Reporting and interpreting the results of a survey • Analyzing paragraphs • Interpreting
• Identifying the reasons for people's preferences • Distinguishing between positive and negative opinions	• "The Aircar and the Lean Machine" (jigsaw reading) • "Los Angeles in 1901" (WB)	Summarizing an interview • Quoting someone
• Understanding questions and answers • Collecting information about someone's achievements	• "Gabrielle Reece" • "Mark Allen—Triathlete" • "No Time for Sports" (WB)	Reporting and interpreting • Interpreting • Quickwriting
• Listening for details about travel destinations • Listening for information to confirm your predictions	• "Three Great Places to Visit" • "My Private Hawaii" • "A Great Place to Hang Out" (WB)	Describing a place • Taking notes in a chart • Getting your reader's attention
• Listening for details about gifts people have received • Listening to people describe the kinds of gifts they give	• "A Gift of Gold" (folktale) • "The Boy Who Cried 'Wolf'" (WB)	Telling a story • Making a story map
• Listening to confirm a prediction • Distinguishing between positive and negative recommendations	• "Four Great Movies" • "'Roses' Fails to Deliver" • "One of the Great Movies of All Time" (WB)	Recommending a movie • Quickwriting • Making a cluster diagram
• Distinguishing between certain and potential consequences • Listening for details to complete a chart	• "How to Calculate Your Life Expectancy" • "Three Good Reasons Not to Be a Workaholic" (WB)	Being Persuasive • Brainstorming
• Listening for details about future plans	• "Two People Who Reached Their Goals" • "Ten Years from Now" (WB)	Describing future plans and dreams • Classifying

Introduction

Integrated English

Integrated English is a four-skills program for adult and young adult students of American English. Comprised of three, two-book courses—*Gateways*, *Transitions*, and *Explorations*—this program takes students from beginner through intermediate levels. Recognizing that students' language learning needs change as they progress from one level to the next, the *Integrated English* program varies its approach to meet students' specific needs at each level.

Transitions

Transitions, the second course in the *Integrated English* program, is for students at a low-intermediate level. It features an innovative topic-based syllabus in which authentic content provides both a context for meaningful language work and a basis for the exploration of interesting adult topics.

Key Features of Transitions

- **Rich content** (photo collages, interviews, first-person accounts, captioned photos, charts and graphs, etc.) that provides students with reasons to confer, ask meaningful questions, seek clarification, share opinions, make comparisons, and agree or disagree.

- **Separate fluency-based and form-based activities.** Separating these activity types makes it clear to students when they can focus on communicating their ideas and when they should be focusing on a specific language structure.

- Fluency-based activities that provide students with **multiple opportunities to recycle** previously studied language structures and vocabulary. In essence, each unit in *Transitions* functions as a review unit of previously studied material.

- **A discovery approach to grammar** that gives students the opportunity to talk explicitly about language, and to ask questions and make and test hypotheses about a particular structure.

- **Task-based activities that integrate the skills of reading, writing, speaking, and listening.** For example, an activity in *Transitions* might ask pairs of students to come up with questions about a photograph, listen for answers to their questions and take notes, read to get more information, and then to relate what they learned to their own lives by completing a chart.

Components of Transitions

- **Student Book.** Each of the 12 units in *Transitions 1* is six pages long. A Strategy Session follows the third, sixth, and ninth units and introduces important conversation management strategies. The Grammar Guide in the back of the book can be used for in-class reference or at-home study.

- **Cassettes and CDs.** All listening activities, pronunciation exercises, conversations, and reading exercises in the Student Book are recorded. This symbol 📼 next to an exercise indicates that it is recorded.

- **Workbook.** The Workbook provides activities and exercises to supplement the material presented in the Student Book. This material can be used in class or done as homework. In addition, the Workbook provides a comprehensive process writing program.

- **Teacher's Book.** The Teacher's Book contains step-by-step suggestions for setting up and carrying out the activities in the Student Book. Background and cultural information related to the topic of the unit as well as Teaching Tips and Expansion Activities give teachers practical suggestions and ideas on how to adapt the material to their own teaching needs.

How Does a Unit in Transitions Work?

Each unit in *Transitions* is organized into two, three-page sections. These three-page sections work as follows:

Presentation, Practice, and Interaction

1st page. The first page of each unit is the Presentation section. The activities in this section introduce the topic of the unit and get students to communicate their ideas using language previously studied.

2nd page. On the second page of each unit, the Practice section asks students to focus on a linguistic feature that came up naturally during the presentation of the unit topic. The activities on this page get students to investigate a particular grammatical structure and to experiment with using it.
Cross-referenced to the Practice page, the Grammar Guide in the back of the book provides additional examples of the target structures, helpful tips on form and usage, plus a form-based exercise for extra grammar practice.

3rd page. The activities on the third page of each unit bring the students back to the unit topic and provide them with opportunities for genuine interaction. These activities give students a chance to "try out" the language structure from the previous page in a meaningful communicative context.

Preview, Exploration, and Expansion

4th page. The second half of the unit begins on the fourth page with a Preview section. The communicative activities on this page get students thinking and talking about a new aspect of the topic while also preparing them for a short reading on the following page.

5th page. A short reading on the fifth page gives students the opportunity to experiment with useful strategies such as reading for specific information and using context to guess the meaning of words. At the same time, the reading provides students with interesting ideas and information that they can react to and talk about.

6th page. The communicative activities on the sixth page of each unit get students to expand on the information in the reading and to apply this information to their own lives. These activities can also serve as a jumping-off point for additional project work and writing activities.

EXPLORE

1. Where will you find these things?
Write the page number.

   a. A unit about customs *page 13*
   b. A unit about gift-giving page 53
   c. A unit about clothing page 21
   d. Strategy Session One page 19
   e. A world map pages 86-87
   f. The Pronunciation Point activity for Unit 8 page 89 (48)
   g. The Grammar Guide for Unit 6 page 96
   h. A list of irregular verbs page 103

2. **True or false?**

   a. There are ten units in *Transitions*. *False. There are 12 units in Transitions.*
   b. Each unit is eight pages long. False. each unit is 3 pages long.
   c. The second page of each unit always contains a blue grammar box. True
   d. Strategy Sessions teach how to keep a conversation going. True.
   e. Each Strategy Session is three pages long. False, each is one page long
   f. There are extra exercises in the Grammar Guide. True.

USEFUL EXPRESSIONS

1. Use the expressions in the box to complete the conversations below.

—What does *cheap* mean?	— How do you spell that?
—How do you pronounce this word?	What's an *intern*?
—Could you repeat that?	—What's this called in English?

(A) *How do you pronounce this word?*
(B) Which one? This one?
(A) Uh-huh. That one.
(B) Caffeine.
(A) what does cheap mean ?
(B) It means *not expensive.*
(A) what's this called in English ?
(B) This? It's called a bulletin board.
(A) I'm sorry. Could you repeat that ?
(B) Sure. Bulletin board.

(A) How do you say ☕ in English?
(B) Coffee.
(A) How do you spell that ?
(B) Coffee? C-O-F-F-E-E.
(A) what's an intern ?
(B) Someone who works for very little money
to get work experience. Interns are often university students.

2. Listen and check your answers.

Topic: Spending time
Language: Getting information
Focus: Questions with do and did

PRESENTATION

1. What did you do yesterday?
   Listen to one person's answer and
   write the missing times.

order

A DAY IN THE LIFE OF AN MTV INTERN

7:00 A.M.
The dog woke me up.

7:05– 7:25 A.M.
Walked the dog.

7:30 –8:00 A.M.
Took a shower. Drank cup
of coffee #1.

8:01– 8:30 A.M.
Got dressed.

8:35 A.M.
Left for work. Stopped at a
nearby coffee bar for coffee
#2 and coffee #3.

9:05 A.M.
Got on the subway.

9:30 A.M.
Arrived at the MTV
office. Got breakfast at
the restaurant downstairs.
Talked with co-workers.

9:40 A.M.– 12:00 P.M.
Worked in the MTV
offices. Drank coffee #4
and coffee #5.

2:00 –2:45 P.M.
Ate lunch—wings
and fries.

2:46– 6:45 P.M.
Worked. Drank
coffee #6.

6:45 P.M.
Finished work.
Got ready to go home.

7:30 P.M.
Arrived home.

8:00 –9:00 P.M.
Watched TV with
friends.

9:15–10:00 P.M.
Had dinner at the
Odessa—really great,
really cheap. Ordered
a cheeseburger, fries,
and a "Coke" with
lemon. Drank coffee #7.

11:00 P.M.– 2:00 A.M.
Went with friends to
hear music at the
Manhattan Center
Ballroom.

2:15 A.M.
Walked the dog. Went
to sleep. (Caffeine has
no effect on some
people.)

*Amanda Block studies television
journalism at New York University.
She also works part time at MTV News.*

2. *Pairs.* What did <u>you</u> do yesterday?
   Tell your partner three things.

1

PRACTICE

1. We asked Amanda Block the questions below. Match our questions and her answers.

> **GETTING INFORMATION:** *Questions with do and did*
>
> | Questions | Answers |
> |---|---|
> | a. Do you like your job? | _D_ Lots of different things. |
> | b. Did you work at MTV last year? | _E_ A little tired. |
> | c. How many days a week do you work at MTV? | _C_ Two days a week. |
> | d. What do you do at work? | _B_ No, I didn't. |
> | e. You went to bed at 2:15 A.M. | _a_ Yes, I love it. |
> | How did you feel the next morning? | |
>
> - Which of the questions above ask something about the past? Which words help you to know? *did / went , last year*
> - Which questions ask for a *yes* or *no* answer? How do you know?
>   **Answers on page 91** *a and b , because it uses do and did*

Why...? How...?
Who...? — Questions — When...?
What...? Where...?

2. *Pairs.* We asked Amanda five more questions.
   Use the words in parentheses to write our questions.

   Question: <u>*Do you live alone?*</u> (*live alone*)
   Answer: No, I don't.
   Question: <u>*who do you live with ?*</u> (*live with*)
   Answer: My sister and my dog.
   Question: <u>*How do you get home from work?*</u> (*get home from work*)
   Answer: By subway.
   Question: <u>*what do you like about new york?*</u> (*like about New York*)
   Answer: Almost everything. You can always find something to do.
   Question: <u>*When did you move to new york?*</u> (*move to New York*)
   Answer: Three years ago.

   Listen and check your ideas.

3. *Pairs.* Test your memory! What do you remember about Amanda Block from page 1? List four things.

   Example:
   She works at MTV.
   She got up at 7:00 A.M.

   Now turn this information into questions. Then see if your classmates can answer your questions.

   Example:
   She works at MTV. → Where does she work?
   She got up at 7:00 A.M. → What time did she get up?

   PRONUNCIATION POINT: *Question intonation*
   Does Amanda Block work?
   When did Amanda Block have lunch?
   Go to page 88.

ASK QUESTIONS

1. *Pairs.* What other questions could you ask Amanda
Block? Add them to the diagrams below.

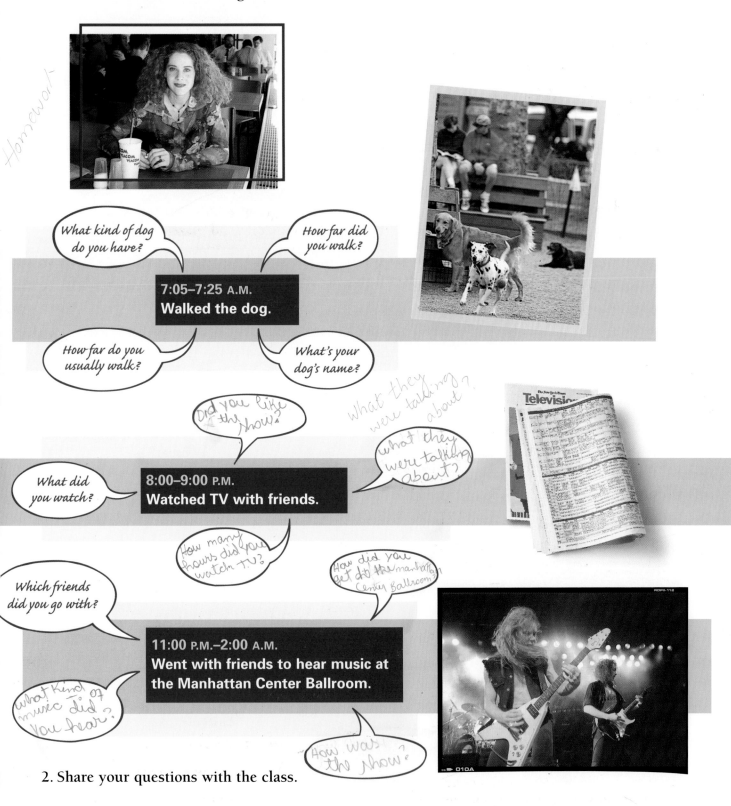

*What kind of dog
do you have?*

*How far did
you walk?*

**7:05–7:25 A.M.
Walked the dog.**

*How far do you
usually walk?*

*What's your
dog's name?*

Did you like
the show?

What they
were talking
about?

*What did
you watch?*

**8:00–9:00 P.M.
Watched TV with friends.**

what they
were talking
about?

How many
hours did you
watch TV?

How did you
get to the manhattan
Center Ballroom?

*Which friends
did you go with?*

**11:00 P.M.–2:00 A.M.
Went with friends to hear music at
the Manhattan Center Ballroom.**

what kind of
music did
you hear?

How was
the show?

2. Share your questions with the class.

SHARE INFORMATION

Pairs. Turn to page 79.

PREVIEW

1. *Pairs.* Where did Greg Sergi and his friend go last summer? What did they do on their trip? Study the photographs and think of five questions. Write your questions in the chart below.

Greg Sergi is a student at a university in the U.S. We asked him about a trip he and his friend took last summer.

"We spent a day at the beach."

"We visited Disney-MGM Studios."

"We went snorkeling."

"We went to Ernest Hemingway's house."

Why...?   How...?

Who...? ——— Questions ——— When...?

What...?   Where...?

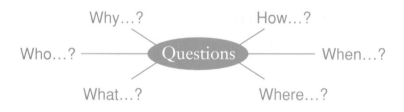

What do you want to know about their trip?	
Questions	**Answers**
1. *What did they do at Disney-MGM Studios?*	learned a lot about movies.
2. DID you go to the beach driving?	Yes, we did.
3. what kind of fish did you see?	hundreds of multi-colored fish and one barracuda.
4. How long did you stay at the beach?	it didn't say.
5. where did you stay at?	we found a cheap hotel.
6. who were with you at Ernest Hemingway's house?	it didn't say.

2. Share your questions with the class.

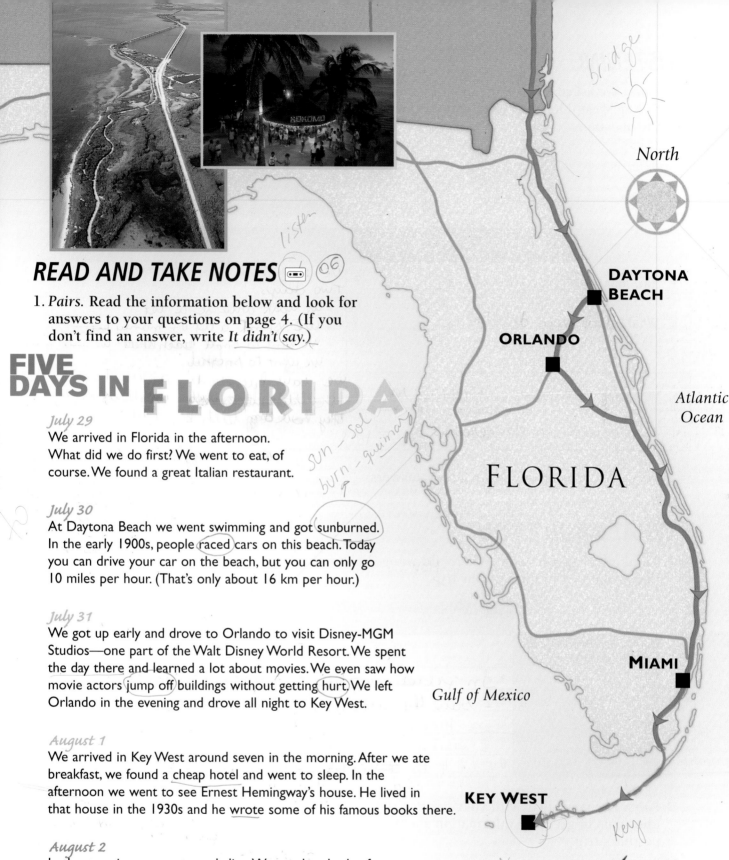

READ AND TAKE NOTES 🔘 06

1. *Pairs.* Read the information below and look for answers to your questions on page 4. (If you don't find an answer, write *It didn't say.*)

FIVE DAYS IN FLORIDA

July 29

We arrived in Florida in the afternoon. What did we do first? We went to eat, of course. We found a great Italian restaurant.

July 30

At Daytona Beach we went swimming and got sunburned. In the early 1900s, people raced cars on this beach. Today you can drive your car on the beach, but you can only go 10 miles per hour. (That's only about 16 km per hour.)

July 31

We got up early and drove to Orlando to visit Disney-MGM Studios—one part of the Walt Disney World Resort. We spent the day there and learned a lot about movies. We even saw how movie actors jump off buildings without getting hurt. We left Orlando in the evening and drove all night to Key West.

August 1

We arrived in Key West around seven in the morning. After we ate breakfast, we found a cheap hotel and went to sleep. In the afternoon we went to see Ernest Hemingway's house. He lived in that house in the 1930s and he wrote some of his famous books there.

August 2

In the morning we went snorkeling. We saw hundreds of multi-colored fish and one barracuda. Key West is a small town but the nightlife is great. Musicians play on the streets and there are lots of good restaurants. We ate dinner and watched the sun go down. Then it was time to go home.

2. Share your answers with the class.

North

DAYTONA BEACH

ORLANDO

Atlantic Ocean

FLORIDA

MIAMI

Gulf of Mexico

KEY WEST

LISTENING

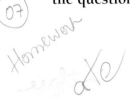

1. *Pairs.* We asked Greg Sergi about his time in Key West, Florida. Listen and complete the questions.

Greg Sergi

[handwritten margin notes: 07, Homework, eighte]

Questions	Answers
a. How long _did you stay there_ ?	We stayed there about 48 hours. Two days.
b. What _did you do there_ ?	• we walked around a lot • we spent a lot of money ~~on the~~ shopping • we went to small beach there, we ate a lot • we went to snorkeling.
c. When you went snorkeling, _what did you see_ ? _were there a lot of fish?_	we saw hundreds of fish tropical fish of all different colors blue yellows we saw a barracuda
d. Are barracudas _is dangerous_ ?	they have big teeth but a little the guy he doesn't so the barracuda will not attack aggressive all

2. *Pairs.* Listen again and write Greg's answers.

[handwritten: Which was the highlight of our stay in Key West. bright]

WHAT ABOUT YOU?

1. Think of a trip you took. Where did you go? List five things you saw or did on your trip.

	My Trip
Where did you go?	I went to Pernambuca Recife and Petrolina
What did you see and do there?	1. In Petrolina I went swimming a river. 2. I saw the fisherman in the morning fishing 3. In Recife I went to the beach. 4. I visited the church. 5. I went to a hippie party with some friends.

2. *Pairs.* Exchange lists with your partner. Ask questions to get more information about your partner's trip.

3. Tell the class about your partner's trip.

[handwritten: our leader the guy who does the tour said that barracudas will not atack. They are not aggresive at all.]

Topic: Lifestyles
Language: Talking about likes and dislikes
Focus: Verb + infinitive/gerund

to sew = sewing company.

Vail, Colorado

PRESENTATION

1. *Pairs.* Would you like to live and work here? Study the pictures and captions. Then answer the questions below.

To shopping comprar

eat all

Bill and Sue Mattison live alone on top of Vail Mountain in Colorado. An average of 750 cm of snow falls here each winter.

They have a TV in their cabin, but they can only get one channel. Luckily, they don't like to watch TV very much.

During the day, the Mattisons are part of a team of 55 ski patrollers in Vail. The ski patrol helps lost and injured skiers.

perdido machucado

In the winter, they sometimes get up at 4:30 in the morning. First they check the weather and measure the snowfall. Then they go out on snowshoes.

medir

- Write

lose lost lost

a. Would you enjoy living on a mountain? Why or why not?
b. Would you like to work for the ski patrol? Why or why not?
c. Would you mind getting only one channel on TV?

ligeria/se importante

2. Report to the class.

I don't mind I don't care

PRACTICE

(handwritten: enjoy / like / hate / wish)

1. Read about the Mattisons'
   likes and dislikes.
   Then tell about yourself.
   Check (✓) Yes or No.

TALKING ABOUT LIKES AND DISLIKES: *Verb + infinitive/gerund*

	YES	NO
a. The Mattisons **enjoy going** outside in cold weather. Do you?	☐	☒
b. They **love getting up** early. Do you?	☐	☑
c. They **like to spend** time alone. Do you?	☑	☐

Add the **bold-faced** words in each sentence to the chart below.

verb + verb/-ing (gerund)		verb + to + verb (infinitive)	
like skiing	dislike working	want to travel	hate to feel cold
mind* living alone	hate staying indoors	need to sleep	*(handwritten: like to spend time)*
(handwritten: love getting up)	*(handwritten: enjoy going)*	love to watch TV	

Which verbs appear in both groups?
Answer on page 92 *(handwritten: like, hate, love)*

---

*NOTICE: Do you mind? = Is it okay with you?
I don't mind. = It's okay with me.

---

2. *Pairs.* Choose words from above to complete these questions.
   (There is more than one way to complete each question.)

   a. Do you *enjoy/like (mind)* getting up early in the morning?
   b. What do you *want/like* to watch on TV?
   c. What do you *want/need* to do on the weekend?
   d. Who do you *enjoy/like* spending time with?
   e. What do you *love/need/want* to do after class?
   f. What do you *dislike/like/enjoy* doing in your free time?
   g. What do you *dislike* doing on a rainy day?
   h. What foreign foods do you *love/like* to eat?
   (handwritten: estrangeiros ... want to)

   (handwritten: — Homework)

   Take turns asking and answering the questions.

   Example:
   (A) Do you enjoy getting up early in the morning?
   (B) No, I don't. What about you?
   (A) *Yes, I do*

3. Complete these sentences.

   a. On weekends, I enjoy *getting up late*.
   b. I dislike *watching TV* in the evening.
   c. I don't mind *ironing*.

   Report your ideas to the class.

I don't mind ironing.

(handwritten: Like to watch TV. Playing)

COMPARE

1. Look at the pictures and compare the questions. In the second question, why does the speaker use *Would* instead of *Do*?

2. Complete each question using *Do* or *Would*.

   a. ___Do/would___ you enjoy studying English?
   b. ___would/Do___ you enjoy working in Canada?
   c. ___Do/would___ you like living here?
   d. ___would/do___ you mind living on a mountain?

3. *Pairs.* Ask and answer the questions above.

   Example:

   Ⓐ Do you ...?   Ⓐ Would you ...?
   Ⓑ Yes, I do.   Ⓑ Yes, I would.
     No, I don't.   No, I wouldn't.

   ▭▭ PRONUNCIATION POINT: *Reduced forms*
   /dəyə/   /wʊdʒə/
   Do you enjoy studying English? Would you enjoy studying German?
   Go to page 88.

LISTENING

▭▭ 1. There are many ways to answer *Yes* or *No.* Listen to these four questions and check (✓) the answers you hear.

Ways to Answer *Yes*		Ways to Answer *No*	
☑ Definitely!	❏ I guess so.	❏ No way.	☒ Me? I don't think so.
☑ Sure!	❏ Kind of.	☒ You must be kidding!	❏ Not really.

▭▭ 2. *Pairs.* Listen again and complete the conversations. Then take turns asking and answering the questions.

   a. Ⓐ Would you like to live on a mountain?
      Ⓑ _Sure_. I'd love it.

   b. Ⓐ Would you like to live alone?
      Ⓑ _ME? I don't think so_. I'd get lonely.

   c. Ⓐ Would you enjoy working for MTV?
      Ⓑ _definitely_.

   d. Ⓐ Would you enjoy traveling around the world by boat?
      Ⓑ _you must be kidding_. I hate the water.

3. *Pairs.* Take turns asking and answering these questions.

   a. Would you like to work seven days a week?
   b. Do you enjoy eating out several times a week?
   c. Would you enjoy working in a bank?
   d. Would you like to spend some time in a foreign country?
   e. Would you like to work in a foreign country?

1. *Pairs.* We collected information about three people with interesting jobs. Work with your partner to find out what they do.

   Person A: Look at this page.
   Person B: Turn to page 80.

2. Person A: What do these people do at work?
   Ask your partner questions to complete the chart.

   Example:
   Ⓐ Does Aaron Chang spend a lot of time outdoors?
   Ⓑ Yes, he does.

What do these people do at work?

	Aaron Chang Yes	Aaron Chang No	Julie Krone Yes	Julie Krone No	Jack Horner Yes	Jack Horner No
spends a lot of time outdoors	✔		✔		✔	
often travels to foreign countries	✔			✔	✔	
gets up early to go to work		✔	✔		✔	
uses a camera at work	✔			✔	✔	
sometimes lives in a tent		✔		✔	✔	
uses a notebook and pen at work	✔			✔	✔	
works with animals		✔	✔		✔	
often works barefoot	✔			✔		✔
often needs to make quick decisions	✔		✔			✔
needs to be in good shape		✔	✔			✔
needs to wear special clothes at work		✔	✔			✔

3. Person A: Now use the chart to answer your partner's questions.

4. *Pairs.* Can you guess each person's job?

   Example:
   Ⓐ I think Julie Krone is a/an …
   Ⓑ Why is that?
   Ⓐ Because she …

photographer
Aaron

architect

police officer

jockey
Julie

scientist
Jack

READ AND TAKE NOTES 🔊

1. Scan the article below and underline each person's job.

Interesting Jobs

Aaron Chang loved to surf, but he didn't think he could make a living doing it. When his father gave him a camera, however, Chang started taking photographs of people surfing. Today, Aaron Chang is one of the best <u>surf photographers</u> in the world. For his job, he travels around the world, surfing in the best places and taking photographs.

Julie Krone rode in her first horse race when she was just 16 years old. Since then, she has won more than 2,800 races. Krone says she loves being a <u>jockey</u> even though it's hard work. On most days, she gets up before sunrise to exercise horses and she rarely gets home before sunset. Being a jockey is also dangerous work. In 1993, Krone fell off her horse during a race and got badly injured. Nevertheless, she loves her job. "I've made enough money so I can do what I love to do every day," she says. "Not many people can say that."

What happened to the dinosaurs? Why did they disappear 65 million years ago? These are questions you should ask <u>scientist</u> Jack Horner. Horner's job is to find and identify dinosaur bones. When Horner is looking for dinosaur bones, he lives in a tent and works from sunup to sundown. His assistants dig up the bones and later, Horner spends hours in his laboratory studying them. According to Horner, it's exciting to be a dinosaur hunter, but it's also hard work.

2. *Pairs.* Read the article again. Look for information to complete the chart.

Name	Job	Interesting lifestyle information
Aaron Chang	Surf photographers.	He likes to surf. He travels around the world.
Julie Krone	JOCKey	she has won more than 2.8000 racers. rode in her first horse race .when she was just 16 years old.
Jack Horner	scientist	he lives in a tent and spends hours in his laboratory studying them.

3. *Pairs.* Would you like to have one of these jobs? Why or why not?

I would/wouldn't like to be a nurse because ...

1) I could to help people sick
2) When I have someone sick, I could take care
3) everyday I could say with is good to have health.

Get together with another pair. Share your partner's answers to the question above.

I could give medicine
help doctors
make the life of sick people easier less painful

INTERVIEW

1. *Groups*. What do you think these people do at work?
Check (✓) your ideas.

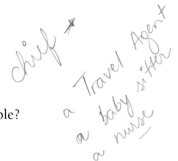

Example:
Ⓐ Do you think a hotel manager spends a lot of time helping people?
Ⓑ Yes, I do.
Ⓒ Me, too.

	spends a lot of time helping people	spends a lot of time working alone	spends a lot of time outdoors	meets a lot of new people	has to talk to groups of people	often makes quick decisions	frequently works with numbers
Hotel Manager	X			X	X	X	
Accountant	X	X					X
Architect		X	X		X	X	
Teacher	X				X		
Doctor	X			X		X	
TV Newscaster		X	X		X		
Police Officer	X		X	X		X	
Chef				X	X	X	

2. *Pairs*. Ask your partner these questions. Check (✓)
your partner's answers.

	YES	NO
a. Do you enjoy helping other people?	☒	☐
b. Do you prefer to work alone?	☐	☒
c. Would you like to work outdoors?	☐	☒
d. Do you like to meet people?	☒	☐
e. Do you feel comfortable talking in front of a group?	☐	☒
f. Do you feel comfortable making quick decisions?	☐	☒
g. Would you mind sitting a lot at work?	☒	☐
h. Do you like to work with numbers?	☒	☐

3. *Pairs*. Study the chart above and your partner's answers.
Choose a job for your partner. Tell your partner why
you chose that job.

> I think you'd enjoy being a _____ because ...

Report to the class.

Topic: Customs
Language: Giving opinions
Focus: It's + adjective + infinitive; gerunds as subjects

PRESENTATION

1. *Pairs.* Study the pictures and captions. Then answer the questions below.

The information below is from the book *Do's and Taboos Around the World.*

"In China, it is polite to sample every dish, and when eating rice, it is customary to hold the bowl close to your mouth."

"In Morocco, shaking hands is customary, although friends will usually greet by kissing."

"In Poland, toasting is common at both formal and informal dinners."

"It is customary to remove your shoes when entering a home in Thailand."

a. Do you usually remove your shoes when you go inside?
b. Do you say anything before you start eating? If so, what?
c. Do you ever greet anyone with a kiss? If so, who?

2. Report to the class.

PRACTICE

1. Read the questions and answer
Yes, No, or *It depends.*

> **GIVING OPINIONS: It's + *adjective + infinitive; gerunds as subjects***
>
> | | YES | NO | IT DEPENDS |
> |---|---|---|---|
> | a. Is it okay to wear shoes in your house? | ☒ | ☐ | ☐ |
> | b. Is it common to shake hands when you meet someone? | ☐ | ☐ | ☒ |
> | c. Is it okay for women to wear pants to work? | ☒ | ☐ | ☐ |
> | d. Is eating with your fingers impolite? | ☐ | ☒ | ☐ |
> | e. Is toasting common at formal dinners? | ☐ | ☐ | ☐ |
> | f. Is being on time important? | ☒ | ☐ | ☐ |
>
> More examples on page 93

2. *Pairs.* Take turns asking and answering questions using words from the chart below.

PRONUNCIATION POINT: *Sentence stress*
Is it okay to smoke in a taxi?
Go to page 88.

Example:

A Do you think it's rude to wink at a stranger?

B Yes, I do. (No, I don't think so.)

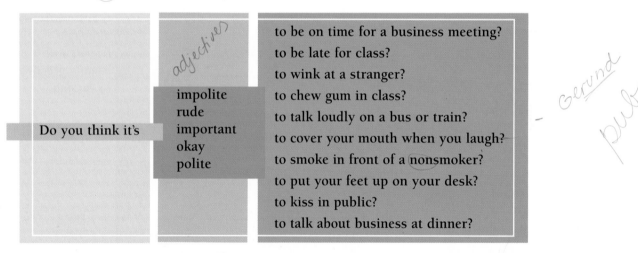

Do you think it's	impolite rude important okay polite	to be on time for a business meeting? to be late for class? to wink at a stranger? to chew gum in class? to talk loudly on a bus or train? to cover your mouth when you laugh? to smoke in front of a nonsmoker? to put your feet up on your desk? to kiss in public? to talk about business at dinner?

3. *Groups.* Group the ideas below. Then add two of your own ideas to each group.

Smoking in a movie theater   Eating with your fingers   Dropping trash on the street
Wearing shorts in public   Holding hands in public   Blowing your nose in public

> **We think...** Eating with your finger,
> Holding hands in public.
> giving gift in special date,
> Kissing friends on the Face in
> public.
> ...is okay.

> **We think...** Smoking in a movie theater,
> Wearing shorts in public
> Dropping thrah on the street,
> Blowing your nose in public,
> Driving and talking on cell phone
> Drinking and driving ...is not okay.

Share your ideas with the class.

LISTENING

(14)

1. We interviewed three students about customs in their countries. Listen and write the questions you hear.

Mahmoud (Saudi Arabia) Ernesto (Mexico)  Yoko (Japan)

Questions	Saudi Arabia			Mexico			Japan		
	Yes	No	It depends	Yes	No	It depends	Yes	No	It depends
a. Is it okay for man and woman to hold hands in public?		X		X					X
b. Is it common for two women to hold hands in public?	X				X				X
c. Is it common for two men to hold hands in public?	X			X				X	

2. Listen again and check (✓) each person's answer.

15 | 16 | 17

SHARE INFORMATION

1. *Pairs.* Person A: Look at this page.
   Person B: Turn to page 81.

2. Person A: Ask your partner questions to complete the chart.

   Example:
   A In the U.S., is it okay to put your feet up on the furniture?
   B Yes, it is.
   A How about in Ecuador? Is it okay to put your feet up there?

IS IT OKAY...	The U.S.		China		Ecuador	
	Yes	No	Yes	No	Yes	No
a. ...to put your feet up on the furniture?	✓			✓		✓
b. ...to arrive early for a party?		✓		✓	✓	
c. ...to ask "How much money do you make?"		✓	✓		✓	
d. ...to ask a woman "How old are you?"		✓	✓			✓
e. ...to use a toothpick in a restaurant?		✓	✓			✓
f. ...to use a cellular phone in a restaurant?		✓	✓		✓	
g. ...to call a teacher by his/her first name?	✓			✓		✓
h. ...to talk to your teacher with your hands in your pockets?	✓			✓		✓

3. Person A: Now use the chart to answer your partner's questions.

4. *Pairs.* How are customs similar and different in these countries? Write three ideas.

   Example:
   In the U.S., it's okay to put your feet up on the furniture, but it's not okay in China.

PREVIEW

1. *Pairs.* Here are some common American
   gestures. Match the pictures and the phrases.

    a. Just a minute.
    b. Come here!
    c. Who, me?
    d. Time out! (Stop for a minute!)
    e. Please be quiet.

What gestures do <u>you</u> use to communicate the same information?

2. *Pairs.* Take turns asking the questions below. Answer
   using <u>your own</u> gestures and body language only.

  3 a. Where's the door?   1 d. What does "sarsaparilla" mean?
  5 b. How was your last vacation?   4 e. Do you like going to the dentist?
  2 c. How many cups of coffee or tea
     did you have yesterday?

3. *Pairs.* We asked this person to answer the same
   questions. Write the letter of each question below
   the appropriate picture.

  1. _D_   2. _C_   3. _A_   4. _E_   5. _B_

**Are his gestures and body language different
from yours? If so, how?**

READ AND COMPARE 18

1. *Groups.* We asked these four people the question below. Read their answers and take notes in the chart.

How do you greet people?

"It depends on the situation. In formal situations, I usually shake hands. And when I meet someone for the first time, I almost always shake hands. And it's important to shake hands firmly. When I greet close friends, I usually give them a hug. For casual friends, I just say 'Hi!' It's a little different for men though. Where I live, it's not so common for male friends to hug each other."
—Sandra (USA)

"In formal situations or when I meet someone for the first time, I shake hands. It's important to shake hands firmly and look the other person in the eye when you greet them. Kissing is perfectly acceptable. It's okay for men to kiss each other, for men to kiss women, and for women to kiss other women."
—Kemal (Turkey)

"In a formal situation or when I meet someone for the first time, I always shake hands. When I greet a male friend, I give him a hug and a pat on the back. When I greet a close female friend, I give her a small hug and a kiss on the cheek. My female friends greet each other the same way."
—Octavio (Venezuela)

"When I meet a friend, I greet them with a wai—I put my hands together in front of my chest and bow slightly—and say 'Sawadee,' which means 'Hello.' In formal situations, some people still use this traditional Thai greeting, but these days more and more businessmen shake hands. Times are changing."
—Noi (Thailand)

Greetings	in formal situations	among friends
in the United States	*shake hands firmly*	*give a hug*
in Turkey	*Shake hands firmly and look the other person in the eye.*	*Kissing is perfectly acceptable between men, men and women, women and women.*
in Venezuela	*Shake hands*	*male friend give a hug and a pat on the back. Female friends give small hug and a kiss on the cheek*
in Thailand	*some people still use this traditional Thai greeting and also shake hands*	*Put the hands together in front of chest and bow slightly and say "Hello".*

2. *Pairs.* Compare greeting customs in these four countries. Find three similarities.

Example:
In formal situations in Turkey and in the United States, people shake hands firmly.

3. *Pairs.* Choose one country in the chart. Role-play a formal greeting. Then role-play an informal greeting.

ROLE PLAY

1. *Groups.* What do you think these people are saying? Study
   their body language and complete their conversations.

2. Listen and complete the conversations.

3. *Pairs.* Practice the conversation with your partner.
   Be sure to use body language.

USEFUL THINGS TO KNOW

1. *Groups.* Choose (✓) one of the categories below.
   List six things a visitor to your country should know.

   ❑ clothing   ❑ eating   ❑ giving gifts

   ❑ dating   ❑ body language ❑ attending a business meeting

   > It's important to
   > be on time for a
   > business meeting.

2. Present your group's ideas to the class.

Strategy Session One

KEEPING A CONVERSATION GOING: ASKING QUESTIONS

1. *Pairs.* Sometimes it helps to ask a <u>general question</u> to get a conversation going. Listen to the conversations below and write the missing questions.

> **GENERAL QUESTIONS**
> What do you mean?
> Really?
> Why is that?/How come?
> How so?
> *(adj)* in what way?

(A) I'd love to go to Key West *[Florida]* someday.
(B) Really? __Why__ __is__ __that__?
(A) Oh, I don't know. I saw some pictures and it looks really beautiful.
(B) Beautiful __in__ __what__ __way__?
(A) Well, it's a small town … and it's near the ocean … and there are lots of trees and flowers … and it's warm.
(B) Mmm, that sounds pretty nice.

(A) I think Amanda Block has an interesting lifestyle.
(B) __How__ __So__?
(A) Well, she lives in New York City and works at MTV.
(B) Yes, but she works long hours.
(A) __What__ __do__ __you__ __mean__?
(B) Well, she leaves home at 8:35 A.M. and she doesn't get back until 7:30 P.M.
(A) You're right. That <u>is</u> a long day.

Now practice the conversations with a partner.

2. *Pairs.* Take turns giving an opinion. Then ask a general question to get a conversation going.

> I think Aaron Chang has an interesting job.

> I wouldn't want to be a jockey.

> I hate to get up early.

> I think it's important to learn a foreign language.

3. *Pairs.* Sometimes it helps to ask a <u>specific question</u> to keep a conversation going. Listen to the conversation below and write the missing questions.

```
        Why...?              How...?

Who...? ————  Questions  ———— When...?

        What...?             Where...?
```

Ⓐ I think Bill and Sue Mattison have a great job.
Ⓑ Really? Why is that?
Ⓐ Well … they live in a beautiful place and they work outdoors.
Ⓑ *Where*   *do*   *they*   *live* ?
Ⓐ On a mountain at a ski resort.
Ⓑ That sounds nice. *what* *do* *they* *do* *there* ?
Ⓐ They work for the ski patrol.
Ⓑ I see. *what* *do* *they* *do* in the summer?
Ⓐ Good question!

Now practice the conversation with a partner.

4. Complete the opinions below.

• I'd really like to go to *California* someday.
• *That* sounds like a nice place to visit.
• I'd hate to *miss it* .
• I think *Eliane* has an interesting life. (*someone you know.*)
• I think *Jonathan* has an interesting job. (*someone you know.*)
• One of my friends loves to *live there* .

5. *Pairs.* Take turns reading an idea from the list above. Then ask general and specific questions to keep your conversation going.

Example:
Ⓐ I'd really like to go to London someday.
Ⓑ Really? Why is that?
Ⓐ *is a nice place*
The City has many interesting places.

Topic: **Clothing**
Language: **Giving reasons**
Focus: **Because, (in order) to, for**

PRESENTATION

1. What do you think of these outfits?
   Share your ideas with your classmates.

Three outfits from the 1700s

a suit of armor

blue robes

a dress with a wide skirt

2. *Groups*. Read each description and answer the questions.

To protect their bodies, soldiers in many parts of the world wore special clothing. This suit of armor was worn in Japan in the 1700s. What special clothing do soldiers wear nowadays?

The Chinese painting above is from the 1700s. The men in blue robes are government officials. The square panel on their robes shows how important they are. Does clothing today help you identify "important" people? How?

Fashionable clothing is sometimes uncomfortable and impractical. In the 1700s, very wide skirts were popular. By the 1740s, some skirts were 5 meters wide. Women had to go through doors sideways! What fashionable clothing today is uncomfortable or impractical?

3. Report to the class.

PRACTICE

**1. Read the questions in the box and put a check (✓) next
to the correct answers.**

GIVING REASONS: Because, (in order) to, for

A. *Why did women wear
very wide skirts?*

- ☐ To look important.
- ☒ Because it was the fashion.
- ☐ For protection from the cold.

B. *Why did government officials
in China wear long blue robes?*

- ☒ To show their profession.
- ☐ Because it was a popular color.
- ☐ For fun.

C. *Why did soldiers
wear armor?*

- ☐ To keep warm.
- ☐ Because it was fun.
- ☒ For protection.

Answers on page 94

**2. Complete each sentence with a reason.
(More than one answer is possible.)**

REASONS

a. Businessmen wear neckties *because it's a custom* *oriental*
To look important
b. Cooks wear aprons *to keep their clothes clean.*
c. People wear coats *to stay warm.*
d. Young people wear jeans *because it's the fashion.*
e. People often wear a hat *for protection from the sun.*
for health reasons.
f. In some parts of the world,
people wear heavy clothing *to stay warm.*

> because it's the fashion.
> because they're comfortable.
> because it's a custom.

> for protection from the sun.
> for comfort.
> for health reasons.

> to look important.
> to stay warm.
> to keep their clothes clean.

3. *Pairs.* Compare answers with a classmate.

Example:
(A) Why do you think businessmen wear neckties?
(B) Because it's a custom.
(A) I think so too. (Hmm. I think it's to look important.)

🔊 PRONUNCIATION POINT: *Syllable stress*

●●● *popular*   ●●● *expensive*

Go to page 88.

**4. *Pairs.* Take turns asking and answering questions
about these clothes.**

Example:
(A) Why do you think people wear sandals?
(B) Because they're comfortable.

Why do people wear ...?	Because it's the fashion.	For protection.	Because it's a custom.	Other
a. sandals	X			*Because they're comfortable.*
b. hats with a wide brim		X		
c. business suits			X	*To look important*
d. earmuffs		X		*to stay warm.*
e. sarongs	X		X	

LISTENING

1. *Pairs.* Write two *Why* questions about the clothing in each picture.

In the Sahara Desert, some people wear long, loose robes. Around their heads and faces they wrap a very long cloth.

Louis XIV, the King of France from 1643–1715, often wore high-heel shoes. The heels on his shoes were red.

Questions	Answers
1. Why _DO people wear long loose robes_ ?	these robes help them to stay cool
Why _do they wear long cloth around their heads and faces?_	to protect their faces from the sunny and windy.
2. Why _did Louis XIV wear high-heel shoes_ ?	Because he was a short man. and to look taller.
Why _do he have long hair_ ?	IT didn't say.

2. Listen for answers to your questions. If you do not hear an answer to your question, write *It didn't say*.

WHAT DO YOU THINK?

1. *Pairs.* Do you and your partner *agree* or *disagree* with these statements?

	We agree.	We disagree.
a. It's important for police officers to wear uniforms. Why? _because they are different of common people common._	☒	☐
b. University students should wear uniforms to class. Why? _because so all know who are students._	☒	☒
c. Clothing should be unisex (the same for men and women). Why? _because it's pratical and for example jeans is comfortable._	☒	☐

Get together with another pair and compare ideas.

2. Report your ideas to the class.

PREVIEW

1. *Pairs.* Listen to the people talking about the shoes below. Listen and put a check (✓) next to the information you hear.

sneakers

snowshoes

sandals

They look ...		They would be good to wear...	
☒ comfortable	☐ expensive	☒ in hot weather	☐ to a dance
☐ uncomfortable	☒ cheap	☐ in cold weather	☒ to school
☐ strange	☒ hard to walk in	☐ in the rain	☐ on a long walk
☒ practical	☐ dangerous to wear	☒ in deep snow	☒ to the beach

2. *Groups.* What do you think of these shoes? Write each person's opinion in the chart.

platform shoes

cowboy boots

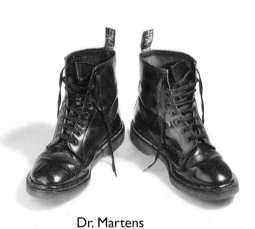

Dr. Martens

What do you think of these shoes?			
name	platform shoes	cowboy boots	Dr. Martens
		strange, uncomfortable	comfortable
	expensive	expensive	Pratical
	good to wear in hot weather	good to wear in cold weather in the rain	good to wear in the rain
	good to wear to dance	hard to walk in Hot weather	good to wear in cold weather
	uncomfortable to walk.		expensive

1. Read the article below and look for information to
complete the chart.

	When were they popular?	Why were they popular?
platform shoes	became popular in the 20th century.	because people to look tall and also because it was the fashion
cowboy boots	became popular in the 1970s.	because it was fancy and practical, with young people and fashionable to wear everyday.
Dr. Martens	in the 1940s	because they were comfortable and fashionable for young women to wear.

FOOTWEAR FADS

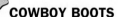

PLATFORM SHOES

In the 1500s, platform shoes became popular in Italy. At first, women wore these shoes to protect their feet and skirts from the wet, muddy roads. Later, very high platform shoes became stylish. Some of these shoes were more than 60 cm high. Women needed help to walk in them. Platform shoes became popular again in the 20th century. In the 1970s, people wore them to look tall and because it was the fashion.

COWBOY BOOTS

Cowboy boots are both fancy and practical. The stitching on the boots is attractive, and it also helps to make the leather stiff. The pointed toe makes it easy to get your foot into the stirrup and the high heel prevents your foot from going through the stirrup. In the 1970s, cowboy boots became popular with young people and fashionable to wear every day.

DR. MARTENS

In the 1940s, a German doctor by the name of Klaus Maertens designed a very comfortable shoe. At first his shoes were popular among elderly people in Germany. Later, workmen in England began buying his shoes because they were so comfortable. Then, in the 1970s, wearing Dr. Martens became the fashion among teenagers. It even became fashionable for young women to wear Dr. Martens with fancy clothes.

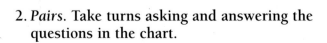

stitching
stirrup
pointed toe

2. *Pairs.* Take turns asking and answering the
questions in the chart.

3. What kinds of shoes are popular today? Why?

VOCABULARY

1. *Pairs.* Person A: Look at this page.
   Person B: Turn to page 82.

2. Person A: Read the sentences under "Across."
   Add the <u>underlined</u> words to the puzzle.

<u>**ACROSS**</u>

4 <u>Slippers</u> are shoes people can wear <u>indoors</u>.
5 A <u>sleeveless</u> dress doesn't have <u>sleeves</u>.
8 <u>Wooden</u> shoes are also called <u>clogs</u>.
9 The pants and shirt that a person sleeps in
   are called <u>pajamas</u>.
10 Women can wear a <u>scarf</u> to cover their hair.
11 People wear <u>gloves</u> to keep their hands warm.

[handwritten annotations: de madera, chanclo, sin mangas, interior, encima de casa, dentro de casa, a mangas, a tamaño, cabría, PJ's]

<u>**DOWN**</u>

1 What can people carry to protect themselves
   from the rain? *UMBRUELAS*
2 In the mud, what can you wear to keep your
   feet warm and dry? *BOOTS*
3 What do motorcyclists wear to protect their
   heads? *HELMETS*
5 What type of footwear is popular in
   hot weather? *SANDALS*
6 What's another word for women's pants? *SLACKS*
7 What do you call a traditional Japanese robe?
   KIMONO

3. Person A: Ask your partner the questions under
   "Down." Add the answers to your puzzle.

Example:
   Ⓐ What can people carry to protect themselves from the rain?
   Ⓑ Umbrellas.
   Ⓐ How do you spell that?
   Ⓑ U-M-B-R-E-L-L-A-S.
   Ⓐ Thanks.

4. Person A: Now answer your partner's questions.

Topic: **Behavior**
Language: **Finding similarities**
Focus: Does too/doesn't either; so does/neither does

PRESENTATION

1. *Pairs.* What are the missing words in this true story?
   Choose words from below and write them on the lines.

life — lives
live — lives

watching worked
drove doing smoked
married see

Jim Lewis

The Story of
JIM LEWIS
and
JIM SPRINGER

Jim Lewis and Jim Springer are identical twins,
but they didn't grow up together. For the first
40 years of their lives, the two Jims didn't
___see___ or talk to each other.

When the two brothers finally met in 1979,
they discovered some amazing similarities in
their lives. Both men ___married___ and divorced
women named Linda. Both men got married
a second time—to women named Betty. Both
men had dogs named Toy. Jim Lewis ___worked___
at a McDonald's restaurant for a while and so did
Jim Springer. They both also worked as police
officers.

The twins also had similar habits and interests.
Both men ___smoked___ cigarettes.
They ___drove___ the same kind of car. Neither
man enjoyed ___watching___ baseball, but they both
liked car racing. Jim Springer liked to build
things and his twin brother <u>did too.</u>
And both of them enjoyed ___doing___
housework.

Jim Springer

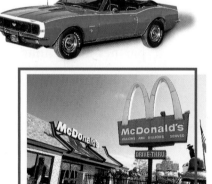

 2. Listen and check your answers. (32)

PRACTICE

1. Read these sentences about Jim Lewis and Jim Springer and check (✓) *That's true, That's false,* or *It didn't say.*

FINDING SIMILARITIES: Both/neither; does too/doesn't either; so does/neither does	That's true.	That's false.	It didn't say.
a. **Both of** them married women named Linda.	☑	☐	☐
b. **Neither of** them can drive a car.	☐	☑	☐
c. Jim Lewis has several children and his brother does **too.**	☐	☐	☑
d. Jim Lewis doesn't work and his brother doesn't **either.**	☐	☐	☑
e. Jim Lewis worked at a McDonald's and **so** did Jim Springer.	☑	☐	☐
f. Jim Lewis doesn't like to build things and **neither** does Jim Springer.	☑	☑	☐

Answers on page 95

2. *Pairs.* Tell about yourself. Decide if these statements are true or false about you and your partner.

		True	False
Likes and Dislikes	a. Both of us like to go to the movies.		✗
	b. Neither of us enjoys playing baseball.	✗	
Habits	c. My partner reads the newspaper every day and I do too. *neither do I* *so do I*		✗
	d. My partner doesn't smoke and I don't either.	✗	
Abilities	e. My partner can drive a car and so can I.	✗	
	f. My partner doesn't speak French and neither do I.	✗	

Example:

(A) Do you like going to the movies?   (A) Can you drive a car?
(B) Yes, I love to. Do you?   (B) No. Can you?
(A) Yes, I do.   (A) Yes, I can.

Now read one of the true statements to the class.

3. *Pairs.* Ask questions to find six more ways you and your partner are similar. Write down what you have in common.

(Do you ...?) (Can you ...?)

Things we have in common	
Likes and Dislikes	I like to sleep and Adriana doesn't either I don't like to drink and neither does Adriana
Habits	I watch TV everyday and my sister does too. I have class everyday and my sister doesn't either
Abilities	My mother doesn't like to travel and I do too Jonathan work everyday and so do I.

Homework

Get together with another pair and compare your answers. Is there anything that <u>all four of you</u> have in common?

(All of us ...?)

LISTENING

1. Listen to these people agreeing and politely disagreeing. Check (✓) the comments you hear.

33

Ways to Agree	Polite Ways to Disagree
☑ So do I.	☑ Really? Why is that?
❑ I do too.	❑ You do? Why is that?
❑ Me too.	❑ Oh? Why is that?
☑ I think so too.	❑ Oh? Why do you think so?
❑ I don't either.	☑ Really? Why not?
☑ Neither do I.	❑ Really? What don't you like about it?

2. *Pairs.* Listen to these people. Do they agree or disagree?

34

- a. They agree.   They disagree.
- b. They agree.   They disagree.
- c. They agree.   They disagree.
- d. They agree.   They disagree.
- e. They agree.   They disagree.
- f. They agree.   They disagree.

boring

PRONUNCIATION POINT: *Sentence stress*

● ·●   ● · ·●
So do I.   *Neither do I.*
Go to page 89.

3. *Pairs.* What do <u>you</u> think of this music? Listen and share your opinions.

25

VOCABULARY

1. *Pairs.* Make a guess! Check (✓) the statements that you think are true about your class.

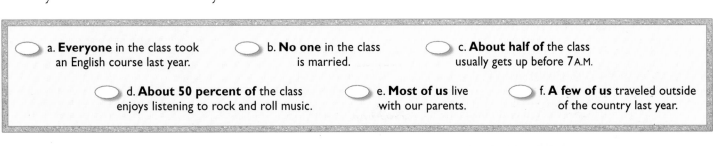

a. **Everyone** in the class took an English course last year.	b. **No one** in the class is married.	c. **About half of** the class usually gets up before 7 A.M.
d. **About 50 percent of** the class enjoys listening to rock and roll music.	e. **Most of us** live with our parents.	f. **A few of us** traveled outside of the country last year.

Use these words with a <u>singular</u> verb	Use these words with a <u>plural</u> verb
• everyone • half the class • no one • everybody • none of us • nobody • fifty percent of the class	• all of us • most of us • a few of us • some of us • many of us • three of us • almost all of us

cuantar

2. Your teacher will read the six questions below. After each question, raise your hand if you can answer *Yes.* Count the people who raise their hands.

- a. Did you take an English course last year?
- b. Are you married?
- c. Do you usually get up before 7 A.M.?
- d. Do you enjoy listening to rock and roll?
- e. Do you live with your parents?
- f. Did you travel outside the country last year?

Were your guesses in Activity 1 correct?

PREVIEW

1. **Read the questions below and check (✓) your answers.**

Bernice Kanner is a writer and researcher. She spent two years interviewing people in the United States for her book Are You Normal? *Below are seven of the questions she asked.*

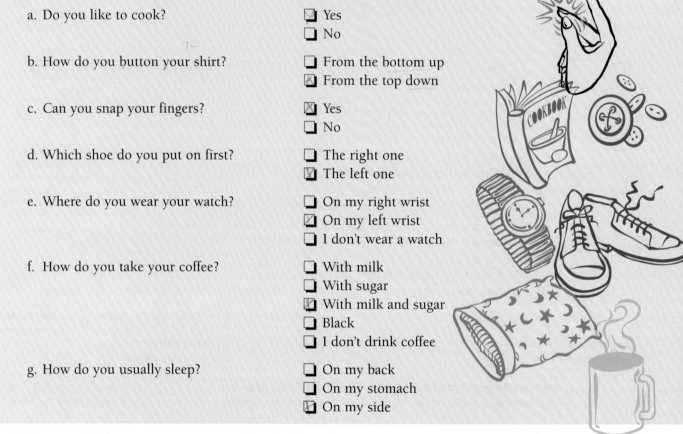

a. Do you like to cook?
☑ Yes
☐ No

b. How do you button your shirt?
☐ From the bottom up
☒ From the top down

c. Can you snap your fingers?
☒ Yes
☐ No

d. Which shoe do you put on first?
☐ The right one
☒ The left one

e. Where do you wear your watch?
☐ On my right wrist
☒ On my left wrist
☐ I don't wear a watch

f. How do you take your coffee?
☐ With milk
☐ With sugar
☒ With milk and sugar
☐ Black
☐ I don't drink coffee

g. How do you usually sleep?
☐ On my back
☐ On my stomach
☒ On my side

2. *Groups.* **Collect your answers and write them in a chart like the one below.**

Question	Person 1	Person 2	Person 3	Person 4
a	yes	yes	yes	no
b	bottom up	top down	top down	bottom up
c				

Summarize your group's answers. Then report to the class.

Example:

> Two of us button our shirts from the bottom up and two of us do it from the top down.

READ AND IDENTIFY 🔊 37

1. What did Bernice Kanner find out about people in
   the United States? The answers below are from her
   book *Are You Normal?* Match the questions she asked
   with the answers she got.

Questions

a. Do you like to cook?

b. How do you button your shirt?

c. Can you snap your fingers?

d. Which shoe do you put on first?

e. Where do you wear your watch?

f. How do you take your coffee?

g. How do you usually sleep?

Answers

Can You snap your fingers?

You'd think everyone could, wouldn't you? But
32 percent of Americans can't. Left-handed
people seem to have more trouble than right-
handed people.

How do you usually sleep?

Twenty-five percent of Americans say they
sleep on their stomach. Fourteen percent sleep
on their back. The rest sleep on their side.

Where do you wear your watch

Most people wear it on their left wrist. Fewer
than two in every hundred don't wear one at all.

Which shoe do you put on first?

It's pretty much a toss-up with just a few more
people putting on the right one first. However,
almost three out of four left-handed people put
on their left one first.

How do you button your shirt?

More than three times as many people do it from
the top down as from the bottom up.

Do you like to cook?

Fifty-six percent of American men and 78
percent of American women say they love to
do this.

How do you take your coffee?

A third of Americans don't drink coffee at all.
Those who do, drink an average of 1.87 cups a
day. Men drink more coffee in a day than
women. Half of all coffee drinkers take it black.

2. *Groups.* Did any of the answers above surprise you?
   Which ones? Why?

LISTENING

1. We asked six people the question below. Listen. <u>Each time</u> you hear one of these answers, put a check (✓) next to it.

38|39|40|
41|42|43|
44|

a couple

> What do you usually carry in your bookbag, purse, or briefcase?

ANSWERS

1✓ 5✓ 6✓ something to read (magazine, newspaper, etc.)	*5✓* something to eat
5¹ 1✓ 4✓ something to write with (pen, pencil, etc.)	*2¹✓ 5✓* keys
	1✓ 2✓ 4✓ money
3✓ 4✓ makeup (lipstick, etc.)	*2✓ 6¹ 4✓* a comb or a hairbrush
	5¹ a cellular phone

2. Listen again. What other answers do you hear? List four things below.

Calculator   Credit Cards

Umbrella   Food / books

3. *Pairs.* Which of these statements describe the people in the survey?

- ☑ Everyone carries a pen or pencil.
- ☐ Most of them carry money.
- ☑ All of the women carry a comb or a hairbrush.
- ☐ No one carries a cellular phone.
- ☑ Some of them carry reading material.

SURVEY

I No body

1. *Pairs.* Think of a survey question to ask your classmates.

   Example:
   What do you usually have for breakfast?

2. Interview five classmates. (Your partner will interview five different classmates.) Record each person's name and answer.

3. *Pairs.* Study the information you and your partner collected. What did you learn from your survey? Write several statements. Then report to the class.

That's all I can think of

Is that it?

anytime

That's it

5 hundred thousand 5
500,00 —
5.000

PRESENTATION

1. **What was the first computer like? What about the first TV? Group these descriptions on the lines below.**

- It weighed 33 metric tons.
- It had a very small screen.
- It only weighed 10 kilograms.
- It cost $500,000.

- It was smaller than a suitcase.
- It was bigger than a small house.
- It cost $100.
- It was built in 1946.

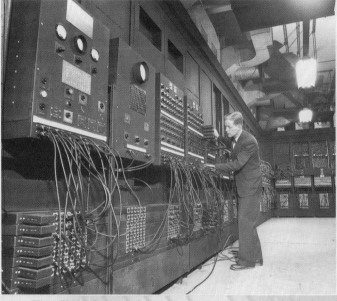

The ENIAC—the first computer

- ☑ *It weighed 33 metric tons.*
- ☑ it cost $ 500,000
- ☑ it was bigger than a small house
- ☑ it was built in 1946

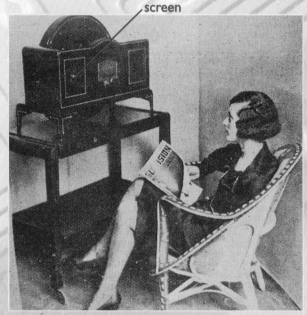

screen

Baird's "Televisor"—the first television

- ☑ It had a very small screen
- ☑ It only weighed 10 kilograms
- ☑ it smaller than a suitcase
- ☑ it cost $ 100.
- It was built 1926

Now compare answers with a partner.

Example:
Ⓐ Which one do you think weighed 33 metric tons?
Ⓑ I think it was the first computer.
Ⓐ Me too. (Really? I think it was the first television.)

2. *Pairs.* Did you group the statements in Activity 1 correctly? Listen and check (✓) the statements.

45/46

PRACTICE

1. Read these sentences about the ENIAC and the Televisor and check (✓)*That's true* or *That's false.*

<table>
<tr><td colspan="2">DESCRIBING DIFFERENCES: Comparative adjectives</td><td>That's true.</td><td>That's false.</td></tr>
<tr><td>a.</td><td>Modern computers are more difficult to use than the old ENIAC.</td><td>☐</td><td>☑</td></tr>
<tr><td>b.</td><td>Today's computers are much smaller than the ENIAC.</td><td>☒</td><td>☐</td></tr>
<tr><td>c.</td><td>The Televisor had a bigger screen than a modern TV.</td><td>☐</td><td>☒</td></tr>
<tr><td>d.</td><td>The Televisor was more expensive than a modern TV.</td><td>☒</td><td>☐</td></tr>
<tr><td>e.</td><td>The Televisor was easier to move than a modern TV.</td><td>☒</td><td>☐</td></tr>
</table>

Look at the bold-faced adjectives above.

- Which comparative adjectives end in -*er?*
- Which comparative adjectives use the word *more?*
- When do we use -*er?* When do we use *more?*

Answers on page 96

> NOTICE: good → better
> A modern TV has a **better** picture than the Televisor.

2. *Pairs.* Predict the missing words. Then listen and complete each conversation.

a. **A** Listen to this! Bicycles in the 1870s were 150 centimeters high.
   B One hundred fifty centimeters! I wouldn't want to fall off a bicycle that tall.
   Yeah, I'm glad bikes are much _smaller_ today.

b. **A** Look at this photograph. It was taken in 1827.
   B Hmm. It's not very clear. Cameras take _better_ pictures today, don't they?

c. **A** Did you know that the first cars could only go about 13 kilometers an hour!
   B Wow! That's a lot _slower_ than cars today.
   slower

3. *Pairs.* Compare the items below. More than one answer is possible.

cheaper   more expensive   faster

larger   more comfortable   more convenient   louder

better   more difficult   easier   worse

Example:
A A camcorder is more expensive than a camera.
B It's also more fun to use.

a. camcorder/camera
b. computer/typewriter
c. a bicycle/a car

d. driving/taking public transportation
e. watching a movie at home/watching
   a movie in a movie theater

LISTENING

1. Choose a word from below to complete each sentence.

a little	a lot
slightly	much
a bit	far

a. I think computers today are ___*a lot*___ more important than they were 30 years ago.

b. I think motorcycles are ___*a bit*___ more dangerous than cars.

c. I think a camcorder is ___*slightly*___ more complicated than a camera.

d. I think an electronic calculator is ___*much*___ easier to use than an abacus.

e. I think regular coffee tastes ___*far*___ better than instant coffee.

Compare answers with a partner.

2. We asked four people the question below. Listen and take notes in the chart.

Example:

Ⓐ Would you rather have a big car or a small car?

Ⓑ Oh, I'd much rather have a small car.

Ⓐ Really? How come?

Ⓑ They're a lot cheaper.

> Would you rather … ?
> Would you prefer to … ?

Would You Rather Have a Big Car or a Small Car?		Big car	Small car	Why?
	1.		✔	*They're a lot cheaper.*
	2.	✔		*because is much safer*
	3.	✔		*big car is a lot more comfortable*
	4.		✔	*They're much more fun to drive*

3. *Groups.* Compare charts. Then ask each other the question above. Report your group's answers to the class.

INTERVIEW

1. Choose (✓) <u>one</u> of the questions below and interview three classmates.

- ❏ Would you rather have a car or a motorcycle? Why?
- ❏ Would you rather communicate by letter or by phone? Why?
- ❏ Would you rather have a camera or a camcorder? Why?
- ❏ Would you rather play a video game or a board game? Why?

2. Report your classmates' answers to the class.

PRONUNCIATION POINT: *Questions of choice*

Would you rather have a big car or a small car?
Go to page 89.

PREVIEW

1. How will cars be different in the future? Check (✓)
   <u>five</u> ways.

   combustion

   I think cars will be _____ in the future.

   ☑ faster   ☐ noisier   ☑ more fuel efficient
   ☑ safer   ☐ heavier *heavy*   ☐ more dangerous
   ☑ quieter   ☑ easier to repair   ☑ more comfortable
   ☐ cheaper   ☑ easier to park   ☑ more expensive
   ☑ smaller   ☑ easier to drive
   ☐ larger

   weight

2. *Pairs.* Take turns reporting an opinion. Listen to
   your partner's response.

   Example:
   Ⓐ I think cars will be smaller in the future.
   Ⓑ So do I. (Really? Why is that?)

3. Look at the pictures. What do you know about these cars?
   What do you want to find out? Write your ideas in the chart.

The Aircar

The Lean Machine

	What do you know about this car?	What do you want to find out about this car?
The Aircar	*It looks like an airplane.* It looks more expensive and more faster than the cars.	*How fast can it go?* Is it easier to park?
The Lean Machine	It looks easier to park and more comfortable	How much is the Lean machine? Is it heavy?

Read your ideas to the class.

READ AND COMPARE 📼 53

1. *Pairs.* Person A: Look at this page.
　　Person B: Turn to page 83.

— 3 meters

2. Person A: Read about this unusual car and answer the questions in the chart.

The Aircar

Would you like to drive to the airport and then fly to another city—without ever leaving your car? Someday you may be able to.

Ken Wernicke is building a car you can both drive and fly. He calls it an Aircar. Wernicke's Aircar has a 10-foot (3 meter) wingspan. That's wide enough to fly but narrow enough to fit on the road. In the air, this unusual vehicle will have a maximum speed of 310 miles per hour (480 km/h). On the highway, it will go 65 miles per hour (100 km/h). With two 50-gallon (200 liter) fuel tanks, this two-person vehicle will be able to travel 1,300 miles (2,100 km) in the air or 2,000 miles (3,200 km) on the road.

	The Aircar	The Lean Machine
How big is it?	*It has a 3-meter wingspan.*	it's smaller an ordinary car
How fast can it go?	in the air per hour 480 Km/h. On the highway per hour 100Km/h.	
How many people can it hold?	it can hold two people	
How is it different from an ordinary car?	This vehicle with 200 liter will be able to travel 2100 Km in the air or 3.200 on the road.	

3. Person A: Ask your partner questions about the Lean Machine to complete the chart.

4. Person A: Now answer your partner's questions about the Aircar.

5. *Pairs.* Use your chart to answer these questions.

a. Which car is faster? The aircar
b. Which car is more useful? The aircar
c. Which car is larger? the aircar
d. Which car is more fuel efficient? the lean machine
e. Which car would you rather buy? Why?

I would buy the aircar because it's faster and I can drive and fly.

LISTENING

1. We asked five people the question below. How did they answer? Listen and check (✓) *Yes, No,* or *I don't know.*

Do you think technology is making our lives better?			
	Yes	No	I don't know.
Person 1	☑	☐	☐
Person 2	☐	☐	☑
Person 3	☐	☑	☐
Person 4	☑	☐	☐
Person 5	☐	☑	☐

Listen again and compare answers with a partner.

2. *Pairs.* What reasons did these people give? Listen again and check the reasons you hear.

1 ☑ Many people have running water and heat in their houses.
4 ☑ Medical care is much better.
2 ☑ We can do things faster, like cooking and washing clothes.
5 ☑ The air is a lot dirtier.
3 ☑ It's easier to communicate with people far away.
☐ Weapons are more destructive.
1 ☑ We don't have to grow our own food.
3 ☑ Our lives are more complicated.

Is technology making our lives better? Group the reasons in the chart below.

Yes, technology is making our lives better.	No, technology isn't making our lives better.
Many people have running water and heat in their houses.	

3. *Groups.* Add six more ideas to the chart. Then compare ideas with the other groups in your class.

38 UNIT 6

Strategy Session Two

KEEPING A CONVERSATION GOING: EXPANDING YOUR ANSWER

1. *Pairs.* Listen to the two conversations. Then answer
the questions below.

①

(A) Did you like the movie?
(B) Yeah.
(A) Was the acting any good?
(B) Yeah, it was okay.
(A) Well, was it a good story?
(B) Uh huh.

②

(A) Did you like the movie?
(B) Yeah, it was great! What did you think?
(A) It was a little difficult to understand, but the acting was terrific.
(B) Yeah, Robert Scott is a really great actor. Did you see him in *High Diver*?
(A) No, I didn't. Is that a new movie?
(B) No, it's about five years old.

- How is the second conversation different from the first?
- In the first conversation, Person B gives only short answers. What effect does this have on the conversation?
- In the second conversation, Person B expands his answers. What effect does this have on the conversation?

2. *Pairs.* Expanding your answers helps to keep a conversation going. Listen and complete each conversation.

(A) Do you have a computer?
(B) No, but ____I'd____ ____love____ ____to____ ____get____ ____one____ someday.
(A) What kind of computer would you like to get?
(B) A Macintosh. I think ____They____ ____are____ ____easier____ ____to use____.
(A) How do you know?
(B) I have a Mac at work. I ____love____ ____use____ ____it____.

(A) Did you have a nice weekend?
(B) Yes, it was pretty good. We ____went____ ____to____ ____the____ ____movie____.
(A) Oh? What did you see?
(B) *Star Wars*. It ____was____ ____really____ ____good____.
(A) Really? What did you like about it?
(B) The special effects. They were fantastic. I ____wouldn't____ ____mind____ ____see____ ____it____ again.

3. Read the questions below and answer *Yes* or *No*.
   Then give more information to expand your answer.

   Example:
   Do you have a job?
   ___*Yes, I do. I work in a restaurant two days a week.*___

   a. Do you usually stay up late?
      No, I don't. I usually go to bed 11:00 PM
   b. Do you watch TV very much?
      No, I don't. I watch around 2 hours
   c. Did you have a nice weekend?
      Yes, I do. I went out with my husband and with some friends
   d. Did you go anywhere yesterday?
      No, I don't. I stayed at home.

4. Use the <u>underlined</u> words to write the next question
   in each conversation. Then read the conversations
   out loud with a partner.

   (A) Do you like soccer?
   (B) Like it? I love it. I <u>play</u> almost every Saturday.
   (A) *where do you play?*

   (A) Do you have a computer?
   (B) No, but I'm going to <u>buy</u> one soon.
   (A) *what will you buy?*
       which

   (A) Would you rather have a big car or a small car?
   (B) I'd rather have a big car. I don't <u>like</u> small cars.
   (A) *Why don't you like small cars.*

5. *Pairs.* Take turns asking questions. Answer *Yes* or *No* and
   give more information to keep the conversation going.

   > Would you like to have an Aircar?

   > Would you like to have a twin brother?

   > Do you like to go clothes shopping?

   > Do you think it's okay to wear shoes in the house?

   > Did you do anything interesting last weekend?

Topic: Sports
Language: Talking about events in the past
Focus: Present perfect

PRESENTATION

1. *Pairs.* Gabrielle Reece is a well-known athlete. Can you guess the missing words in this paragraph about her?

Gabrielle Reece

In the past two years, Gabrielle "Gabby" Reece has rock-climbed on a mountain in France, driven a race _car_ in Gainesville, Florida, and parachuted out of an _airplane_ 12,000 feet (4,000 meters) above San Diego, California.

Why would the six-foot, three-inch (192 cm) beach volleyball star do all that scary stuff?

"I'm not a thrill-seeker," says Gabby. "I'd rather go to the _movies_. But I have a job with the television show *MTV Sports* on which I do a different _sports_ every week.

"Some of the stuff I do on the show is scary and difficult," she says. "But I'm willing to look like a knucklehead on TV while I try it."

2. *Pairs.* Listen and check your guesses.

3. *Pairs.* Ask your partner the questions below.

   a. Have you ever parachuted out of an airplane?
   b. Have you ever played volleyball?
   c. What's the most difficult sport you've tried?
   d. What's the scariest sport you've tried?

PRACTICE

1. Read each pair of sentences and answer the questions below.

> **TALKING ABOUT EVENTS IN THE PAST:**
>
> | **Present Perfect** | **Simple Past** |
> |---|---|
> | a. Gabrielle Reece **has tried** many different sports. | Last year Gabrielle Reece **tried** 15 different sports. |
> | b. She's **gone** rock climbing several times. | She **went** rock climbing two years ago. |
> | c. **Have** you ever **played** volleyball? | **Did** you play volleyball when you **were** a child? |
> | d. What team sports **have** you **played**? | What team sports **did** you **play** in high school? |

- Look at the verbs in each pair of sentences. How are they different?
- Which sentence in each pair tells about a specific time in the past? *both*
  What words in each sentence help you to know?

Answers on page 97

> A list of past participles appears on page 103.

03

2. Complete these questions using the correct form of the verb *play*. Then listen and check your ideas.

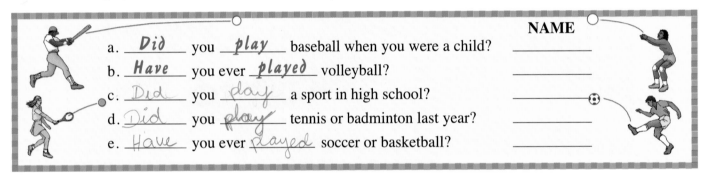

                                                   NAME

a. __*Did*__ you __*play*__ baseball when you were a child? _____

b. __*Have*__ you ever __*played*__ volleyball? _____

c. __*Did*__ you __*play*__ a sport in high school? _____

d. __*Did*__ you __*play*__ tennis or badminton last year? _____

e. __*Have*__ you ever __*played*__ soccer or basketball? _____

Talk to different classmates. Find someone who answers *Yes* to each question above. Write that person's name next to the question.

Jon

Ⓐ Did you play baseball when you were a child?

Ⓑ Yes, I did.   **Ⓑ** No, I didn't.

Ⓐ Have you ever played volleyball?

EDU

Ⓑ Yes, I have.   **Ⓑ** No, I haven't.

VOCABULARY

1. Write about yourself. Complete the sentences below with the name of a sport and the correct verb.

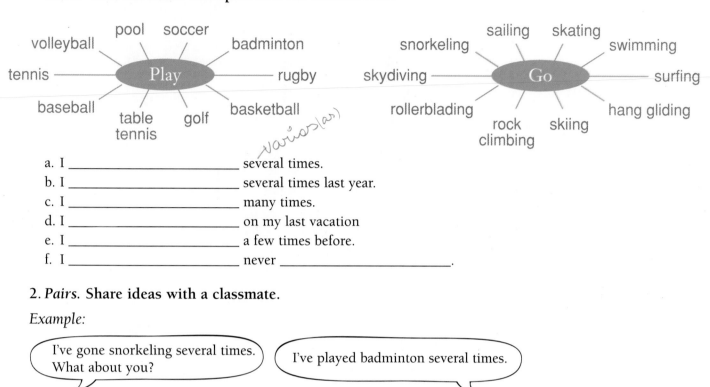

volleyball
pool   soccer   badminton
tennis ——— Play ——— rugby
baseball
table   golf   basketball
tennis

varios(as)

snorkeling   sailing   skating   swimming
skydiving ——— Go ——— surfing
rollerblading   hang gliding
rock   skiing
climbing

a. I _____ several times.
b. I _____ several times last year.
c. I _____ many times.
d. I _____ on my last vacation
e. I _____ a few times before.
f. I _____ never _____.

2. *Pairs.* Share ideas with a classmate.

Example:

> I've gone snorkeling several times. What about you?

> I've played badminton several times.

INTERVIEW 04|05|06|07

1. Listen to the four conversations and add the missing words to complete the diagram.

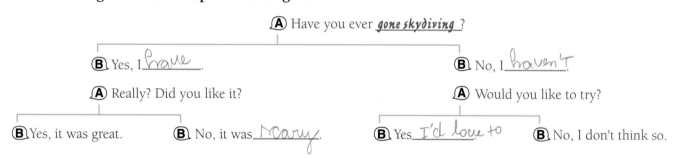

(A) Have you ever *gone skydiving* ?

(B) Yes, I *have* .

(A) Really? Did you like it?

(B) Yes, it was great.   (B) No, it was *lousy*.

(B) No, I *haven't*

(A) Would you like to try?

(B) Yes *I'd love to*   (B) No, I don't think so.

2. *Pairs.* Ask your partner about three other sports.

3. *Pairs.* Find a sport your partner has tried. Then ask three more questions about your partner's experience with the sport.

Example:
(A) Have you ever gone skating?
(B) Yeah, several times.
(A) Is it hard to do?
(B) Well, at first it's kind of hard.
(A) Hard in what way?
(B) _____

PRONUNCIATION POINT: *Unstressed words*

08

How many words do you hear?
Go to page 89.

PREVIEW

1. *Groups.* What is the "Hawaii Ironman?" Look at these photographs and decide if the statements below are true or false.

These photographs were taken at the Hawaii Ironman.

	We think that's true.	We think that's false.
a. The Hawaii Ironman is a race; the fastest person wins.	☒	☐
b. A lot of people compete in the Hawaii Ironman.	☒	☐
c. The Hawaii Ironman is a triathlon; competitors participate in three sports.	☒	☐
d. In the Ironman, competitors swim, run, and surf.	☐	☒
e. Only men compete in the Hawaii Ironman.	☐	☒

09

2. Listen and check your ideas.

LISTEN AND READ

10

1. Mark Allen has won the Hawaii Ironman competition five times. Choose <u>one</u> of the questions below. Then listen for the answer.

a. What sport did Mark Allen play as a child? *swimming*
b. How many times has he won the triathlon in Nice, France? *ten times*
c. Did he win his first triathlon? *No, he did*
d. How many kilometers does he run each year? *2,500 miles (4,000 km)*
e. What does he like to do in his free time? *surf and take nature photographs*

2. Share your answer with your classmates. Then read the article on page 45 and <u>underline</u> the answers to the questions above.

Mark Allen

MARK ALLEN — TRIATHLETE

As a kid in California, Mark Allen didn't have much time to go to the movies or hang out at the mall.[1] "My entire life was swimming and school," he says.

Allen began competing on swim teams when he was ten. He swam with his team for about an hour a day before school.

Allen became such a good swimmer that after high school he competed on his college team. He graduated from the University of California at San Diego in 1980 with a degree in biology.

Two years later, Allen watched the Ironman Triathlon on television. The Ironman is held in Hawaii every year. Competitors must swim 2.4 miles (3.8 km), bike 112 miles (179.2 km), and run a 26.2-mile (41.9 km) marathon. Allen wanted to try it.

He bought a racing bike and running shoes, and started training. He soon found that he was even better at cycling and running than he was at swimming. Just a few months later, Allen entered his first triathlon. He swam, biked, and ran his way to a fourth-place finish.[2]

Allen is now the best triathlete in the world. He has won the Ironman Triathlon five straight times.

Allen is also a ten-time winner of the Nice Triathlon in Nice, France — one of the most important triathlons in the world. That race is made up of a 2.5-mile (4 km) swim, a 74.4-mile (119 km) bike ride, and a 19.8-mile (31.7 km) run.

Allen trains about six hours a day, seven days a week, from January through October. He runs about 2,500 miles (4,000 km) per year, swims about 450 miles (720 km) and bikes about 15,000 miles (24,000 km).

Why does Allen enjoy such a hard sport? "It's just an extreme challenge,"[3] he says.

Allen stops training in November and December so that his body can rest. In his spare time, he likes to surf and take nature photographs.

But for ten months a year, the triathlon is Allen's favorite activity.

"Triathlon is something that I first and foremost enjoy,"[4] he says. "I love the training. I love the traveling. I love the racing. The success has come because of that."

---

[1] **hang out at the mall:** spend his free time at the mall
[2] **ran his way to a fourth-place finish:** finished in fourth place
[3] **It's just an extreme challenge:** It's fun because it's hard.
[4] **Triathlon is something that I first and foremost enjoy:** I do it because I enjoy it.

3. *Pairs*. Write two true and two false sentences about Mark Allen. Have your classmates identify the false sentences and correct them.

GET THE DETAILS

1. How could you continue these conversations?
   Think of different questions you could ask to get
   more information.

   (A) What sports have you tried?

   (B) Volleyball and swimming.

   (A) *what other sport would* ?
   you like to do?

   (A) What sports do you like
   to watch?

   (B) Gymnastics and auto racing.

   (A) *snorkling* ?

2. *Pairs.* Ask your partner the questions below. Then
   ask questions to get more information.

Questions	Answers	Details
▶ What sports have you tried?		
▶ What sports do you like to watch?		
▶ What sports would you like to try someday?		

   Example:
   (A) What sports have you tried?
   (B) Baseball, golf, and tennis.
   (A) Which one do you like best?
   (B) Golf.
   (A) Why golf?
   (B) *it's exciting*

3. Get together with another pair.
   Tell them about your partner's interests in sports.

   *My partner has played tennis and volleyball. She has also done
   a lot of swimming and jogging. Her favorite sport is volleyball
   because she likes team sports. She plays volleyball now
   about once a week.*

Topic: **Places**
Language: **Describing places**
Focus: **Superlative adjectives**

PRESENTATION

1. We asked a travel agent to suggest some interesting places to visit. Here are three of his suggestions.

Rome

Three Great Places to Visit

Bali

Antarctica

Get together with a partner. Match each description to one of the places. Write *A*, *B*, or *R*.

_B_ It's never really cold there.
_A_ It's the windiest place in the world.
    ventoso
_R_ It's noisy and crowded.
_B_ It has some beautiful beaches.
_R_ It's one of the most historic cities in the world.

_R_ There are lots of wonderful old buildings.
_B_ It's a great place to relax.
_A_ It's a good place to see penguins.
_B_ There are a lot of beautiful temples there.

2. Listen to the travel agent's description of each place and check your ideas.

3. *Pairs.* Which of these places would you like to visit most? Why? What about your partner?

I'd like to visit _Rome_ most because ...

PRACTICE

1. Complete these sentences. Write *Antarctica,*
   Bali, or *Rome.* Then listen and check your ideas.

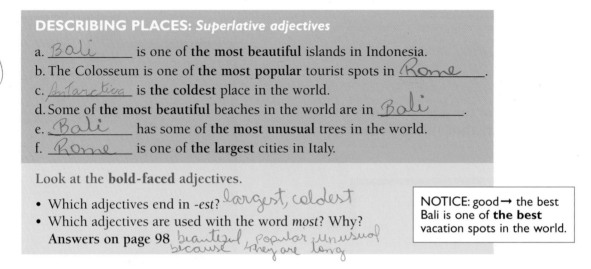

DESCRIBING PLACES: *Superlative adjectives*

a. _Bali_ is one of **the most beautiful** islands in Indonesia.

b. The Colosseum is one of **the most popular** tourist spots in _Rome_.

c. _Antarctica_ is **the coldest** place in the world.

d. Some of **the most beautiful** beaches in the world are in _Bali_.

e. _Bali_ has some of **the most unusual** trees in the world.

f. _Rome_ is one of **the largest** cities in Italy.

Look at the **bold-faced** adjectives.

- Which adjectives end in *-est?* largest, coldest
- Which adjectives are used with the word *most?* Why?
  Answers on page 98 beautiful, popular, unusual
  because they are long

NOTICE: good → the best
Bali is one of **the best**
vacation spots in the world.

2. *Pairs.* Complete these sentences with places
   in your country.

a. Fernando de Noronha is one of the most beautiful places in the country.

b. Campos do Jordão is one of the most popular tourist spots here.

c. The coldest part of the country is in the (north/south/east/west).

d. One of the best places to go swimming around here is Ilhabela.

e. The largest city in the country is São Paulo.

f. We think that PORTO SEGURO is one of the best vacation spots. lugar, local

Compare ideas with another pair.

PRONUNCIATION POINT: *Sentence stress*
Bali is one of the most beautiful places in the world.
Go to page 89.

3. *Pairs.* Think of different ways to complete the
   sentence below. Use words from the list or
   think of your own.

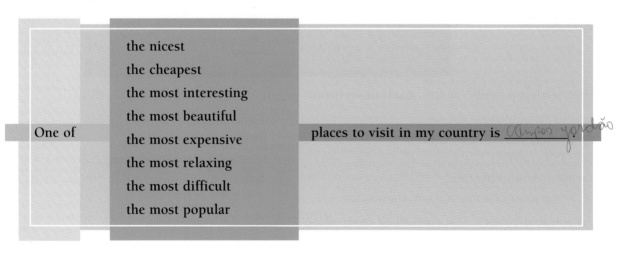

	the nicest	
	the cheapest	
	the most interesting	
	the most beautiful	
One of	the most expensive	places to visit in my country is Campos Jordão
	the most relaxing	
	the most difficult	
	the most popular	

Compare ideas with your classmates.

IDENTIFYING PLACES

1. Complete the questions below using the adjectives in parentheses.

The largest shopping mall in the world has more than 800 stores.

Redwood trees can grow to a height of 110 meters.

The smallest country in the world is surrounded by the city of Rome.

a. Where's _____the biggest_____ shopping mall in the world? (*big*) CANADA

b. Where are __the tallest__ trees in the world? (*tall*) U.S.A

c. What's __the smallest__ country in the world? (*small*) U. City

d. Which country is __the most popular__ tourist destination in the world? (*popular*) FRANCE

e. Where's __the older__ university in the world? (*old*) MOROCCO

f. Where's __the most highly populated__ city in the world? (*highly populated*) MEXICO

g. Where was __the most highly populated__ city in the world 100 years ago? (*highly populated*) England

h. Where's __The busier__ airport in the world? (*busy*) CHICAGO

i. Where's __the longer__ bridge in the world? (*long*) JAPAN

2. *Pairs.* Take turns asking and answering the questions above. Choose an answer from the countries below.

Example:

Ⓐ Where's the biggest shopping mall in the world?

Ⓑ I think it's in Canada. What do you think?

Ⓐ I think you're right. (Canada? I think it's …)

chicago

15,16,17,18,19,20,21,22,23

Canada	the United States	England	Morocco
France	Mexico	Japan	Vatican City

3. Compare ideas with the other groups. Then listen and check your answers.

WHAT ARE THE FACTS?

1. *Pairs.* Think of five facts about <u>your</u> city or country.

Example:
The tallest building is …
The largest university is …

On another piece of paper, turn these facts into questions.

Example:
What's the tallest building in town?
What's the largest university in the country?

2. Exchange questions with another pair. See if they can answer your questions.

PREVIEW

1. *Pairs.* These photographs show seven places in Hawaii.
   Match each picture to one
   of the sentences below.

c.

The Broke the Mouth Cafe

b.

The Hanakapiai Trail

a.

Hana

e.

Polihale Beach

f.

The Halawa Valley

d.

Kawaikoi Stream

The Academy of Art

Haena **b**

OAHU

d

g

KAUAI

Honolulu

e

c

f

MOLOKAI

_D_ A trail winds along this stream. *trilha* *reacho, corrego*

_a_ This is a typical old Hawaiian town.

_B_ There are mountains on one side of this trail and the ocean on the other.

_G_ This museum has a great collection of Japanese art.

_F_ You can swim in the ice-cold water under this waterfall.

_E_ The beach here is a mile long.

_C_ This place has the best food in Hawaii.

2. *Pairs.* Think of one thing you can do in each of
   these places and report to the class.

READ AND IDENTIFY

1. Match each description below with a place on page 50. Write the letter of the place in the box.

Susanna Moore grew up in Honolulu and writes novels about the Hawaii of her childhood. Below are some of her favorite places in Hawaii.

My Private Hawaii

"In the mountains of Kokee on Kauai, a trail winds along a stream, through stands of bamboo, cedar, orchids, and ferns. It is the most romantic, most perfect walk in Hawaii."

"This small, light-filled museum has an especially ravishing[1] collection of Japanese art. My father, who is a doctor, used to leave me there in the hot, hot afternoons while he went to work."

"This is the loveliest, most Hawaiian town in the islands. It is verdant,[2] tropical, and the place of many old legends."

"This is the easternmost point of Molokai. There are two waterfalls at the back of the valley with sacred[3] bathing pools of ice-cold water."

"This is a mile-long beach at the westernmost end of Kauai. The sand here is so hot that you must wear shoes to walk to the water. At the north end, where I like to swim, are big sea turtles and sometimes sharks."

"This trail begins at Haena on the island of Kauai. It's a narrow, difficult trail with mountains on one side and the ocean on the other. During the rainy season it's especially dangerous. It once took me four hours to crawl on my hands and knees in the rain the last half-mile."

"This place has the best local food in the islands. The name is pidgin English[4] for food so good that the mouth breaks with joy. Like pidgin, the food here is a combination of cultures— Chinese, Hawaiian, Portuguese, Japanese."

---

[1] **ravishing:** very beautiful
[2] **verdant:** very green
[3] **sacred:** connected with religion
[4] **pidgin English:** a language made of English and another language

2. Which of these places would you like to visit most? Tell a classmate.

LISTENING

1. In each of these conversations, someone makes a suggestion.
   Read the conversations and predict the missing words.

(25)
  A Can you think of a good _____*place*_____ to spend a rainy afternoon?
  B Have you ever been to the Academy of Art?
  A No, I haven't. What's it like?
  B It's _*small*_ and beautiful. And it has a great collection of Japanese art.

(26)
  A Do you know a _____*good*_____ beach around here?
  B Have you ever been to Polihale?
  A No, I haven't. What's it like?
  B The sand is _*hot*_ but it's a really beautiful beach.

(27)
  A Do you know a good _*restaurant*_ around here?
  B Have you ever been to Broke the Mouth Cafe?
  A No, I haven't. Is it any good?
  B Yeah, it has the _*best*_ local food in Hawaii.

2. Listen and check your ideas. Then read the
   conversations out loud with a partner.

WHAT'S YOUR SUGGESTION?

1. *Groups.* Choose (✓) one kind of place from the list below.

❒ *good places to buy clothes*   ❒ *good restaurants*   ❒ *interesting towns to visit*
❒ *good places to listen to music*   ❒ *good places to go in the evening*   ❒ *good places to go swimming*
❒ *good places to go for coffee*   ❒ *good places to go for a walk*   ❒ *good places to go on a date*
❒ *good museums*

2. Talk to different classmates. Get their suggestions
   for the kind of place your group chose. Write their
   ideas in the chart.

Example:
  A Can you think of a good place to buy clothes?   **A** Do you know a good museum?
  B Have you ever been to …?   **B** Have you tried …?

Name of the place	Why is it good?	Who suggested it?

3. *Groups.* Get together with the people in your group and share the information from your charts.

Topic: Gift-giving
Language: Identifying
Focus: Count/Noncount nouns

PRESENTATION

1. *Pairs.* What's happening in this painting? Look carefully and then answer the questions below.

a. What special occasion might these people be celebrating? Why do you think so?
b. When was the last time you gave someone a gift? What was the occasion?

2. *Pairs.* We asked people the questions below. Listen and draw a line to connect their answers.

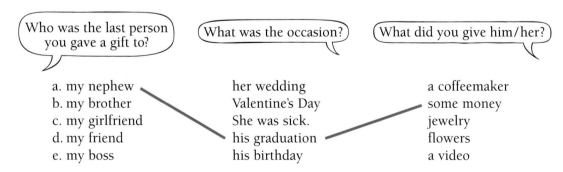

(Who was the last person you gave a gift to?)   (What was the occasion?)   (What did you give him/her?)

a. my nephew	her wedding	a coffeemaker
b. my brother	Valentine's Day	some money
c. my girlfriend	She was sick.	jewelry
d. my friend	his graduation	flowers
e. my boss	his birthday	a video

3. *Pairs.* Take turns asking and answering the questions.

PRACTICE

1. *Pairs.* Answer the questions in the box.

IDENTIFYING: *Count/Noncount nouns*

Count Nouns	Noncount Nouns
a. Do you think a **camera** is a good gift?	d. Do you think **food** is a good gift?
b. Are **flowers** a good gift?	e. Is **money** a good gift?
c. Have you ever given someone **a sweater**?	f. Have you ever given someone **jewelry**?

Now answer the questions below. Check (✓) *Count Nouns* or *Noncount Nouns.*

	Count Nouns	Noncount Nouns
• Which nouns can you use with *a* or *an*?	❏	❏
• Which nouns have a plural form?	❏	❏
• Which nouns do you always use with a singular verb?	❏	❏

Answers on page 99

NOTICE:
Some candy **is** …
A box of candy **is** …
Two boxes of candy **are** …

2. Write *C* next to the count nouns. Write *NC* next to the noncount nouns.

NC money	___ crystal	___ concert tickets	___ earrings
___ flowers	___ clothing	___ a bottle of wine	___ luggage
___ CDs	___ fruit	___ a magazine subscription	___ a video
___ a bracelet	___ a basket of fruit	___ a stuffed animal	___ a scarf
___ a box of candy	___ a good pen	___ a necklace	___ furniture

Compare ideas with your classmates.

3. *Pairs.* Think about a gift you have received and complete the sentence below.

🔊 PRONUNCIATION POINT: *Final -s*

/s/   /z/   /ɪz/
books   flowers   watches

Go to page 90.

_____ gave me _____.
   who?   what?

Read your sentence to your partner and answer any questions your partner has.

Example:
Ⓐ Last year my grandmother gave me some jewelry for my birthday.
Ⓑ Really? What kind of jewelry?
Ⓐ A necklace. It's really beautiful.
Ⓑ What does it look like?
Ⓐ _____

Report to the class.

LISTENING

1. Choose a gift to complete each of these sentences.

GIFT-GIVING DOS AND DON'TS

a. I wouldn't give _____ to someone who is sick.

b. When you go to someone's house for dinner, it's nice to take _____.

c. I think _____ would be a nice wedding gift for a friend.

Compare answers with a partner.

Example:

Ⓐ I wouldn't give candy to someone who is sick.

Ⓑ Neither would I. (Really? Why is that?)

2. Listen and list the gifts each person suggests.

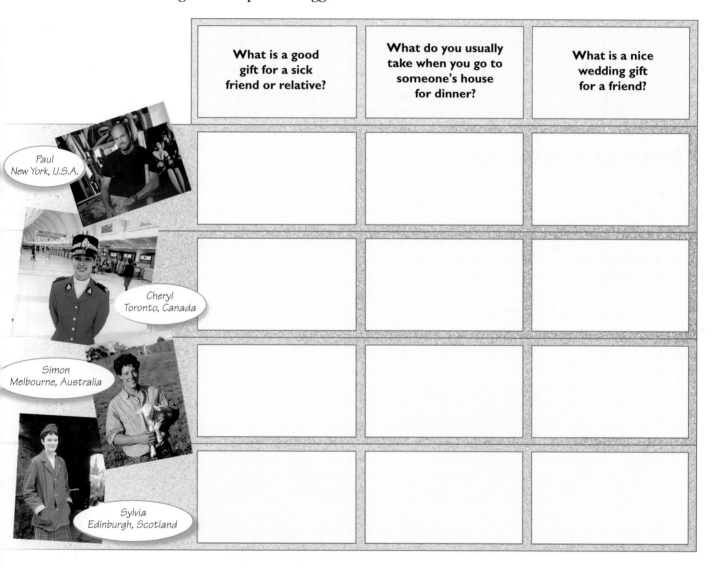

	What is a good gift for a sick friend or relative?	What do you usually take when you go to someone's house for dinner?	What is a nice wedding gift for a friend?
Paul New York, U.S.A.			
Cheryl Toronto, Canada			
Simon Melbourne, Australia			
Sylvia Edinburgh, Scotland			

3. *Pairs.* **How is gift-giving similar and different in these countries? Report to the class.**

Example:

All four people said …   In Australia …, but in …

PREVIEW

1. *Pairs.* The pictures on pages 56–57 show scenes from the story "A Gift of Gold." Find the items below in the pictures. Write the number of the picture or pictures.

	Picture(s)
a. a man who is picking fruit from a tree	*1*
b. an orange piece of fruit called a persimmon	___
c. an enormous, or very large, persimmon	___
d. a very important person	___
e. a large nugget, or piece of gold	___
f. a large animal called an ox	___

Report your findings to the class.

2. *Groups.* Use context (the surrounding words and ideas) to guess the meaning of the **bold-faced** words.

   a. "Mr. Kim watered the tree and soon tiny persimmons appeared on its **branches**."
   b. "When the persimmons were **ripe**, Mr. Kim picked them and gave them to his neighbors."
   c. "Mr. Kim wrapped up the largest persimmon and **set out** for the city to give it to the King."

READ AND RESPOND

1. Read part 1 of the story and look for answers to the questions below.

> • What is Mr. Kim like? What is Mr. Park like?
> • What did Mr. Kim do with the largest persimmon?
> • What did the King do when Mr. Kim gave him the persimmon?
> • Why did Mr. Park buy an ox?

A Gift of Gold (part 1)

1

A long time ago, there lived two men by the name of Kim and Park. Mr. Kim was very generous but Mr. Park was exceedingly greedy.

Next to Mr. Kim's house there was a dying persimmon tree. He watered it every morning and evening, and it grew into a strong, healthy tree. Then, to everyone's surprise, tiny persimmons appeared on its branches.

When the persimmons were ripe, Mr. Kim picked them carefully and shared them with his neighbors. Then he carefully wrapped up the largest persimmon and set out for the city to give it to the King.

The King looked in disbelief when his secretary placed the persimmon before him. "I've never seen such a large persimmon. It's magnificent. The man who grew it deserves a gift. Is there anything as big as this among the gifts I've received lately?"

"Yes, Your Majesty, there is. But, Your Majesty, it's very valuable," said the King's secretary.

"Well, aren't you going to tell me what it is?," asked the King.

"Yes, of course, Your Majesty. It's just that ... well, it's a gold nugget."

"Well, that's no problem. Give it to the man at once."

So it was that Mr. Kim returned home with an enormous gold nugget. News of his good fortune spread quickly through the village.

The greedy Mr. Park was very jealous of Mr. Kim. He decided to take the King something so that he too would get a gold nugget. He pondered what to take. Finally, he sold his house and land in order to buy an ox. Then, with dreams of a gold nugget as big as an ox, he set out to visit the King.

To be continued …

🔊 2. *Pairs.* Compare your answers. Then listen to the recorded version of the story.

ROLE PLAY

1. Listen to this conversation between the King and his secretary.

The King: *(looking very surprised)* I've never seen such a large persimmon. It's magnificent! The man who grew it deserves a gift. Is there anything as big as this among the gifts I've received lately?

Secretary: Yes, Your Majesty, there is. But, Your Majesty, it's very valuable.

The King: Well, aren't you going to tell me what it is?

Secretary: Yes, of course, Your Majesty. It's just that … well, it's a gold nugget.

The King: Well, that's no problem. Give it to the man at once.

2. *Pairs.* Practice the conversation with a partner. Remember to use body language.

3. *Pairs.* Role-play the scene for your classmates.

GUESS THE ENDING!

1. *Pairs.* Work together to answer the questions below.

a. What do you think the King says when he receives the ox from Mr. Park?

_____

_____

b. Do you think the King gives Mr. Park a gift? If so, what is it?

_____

_____

c. At the end of the story, do you think Mr. Park will be happy or sad?

_____

_____

Get together with another pair and share ideas.

2. Listen for answers to the questions above.

3. Turn to page 84 and read the end of the story.

Strategy Session Three

KEEPING A CONVERSATION GOING: USEFUL EXPRESSIONS

1. *Pairs.* Sometimes people use the expressions below to show interest in what the other person is saying. Listen to the conversation and write the missing expressions.

> **USEFUL EXPRESSIONS**
> Uh huh ...   I see ...   Oh?
> Hmm ...   Interesting ...   Really?

(A) I'd really like to go to Hawaii someday.
(B) ___*Oh?*___ Why is that?
(A) Well for one thing, the beaches are beautiful.
(B) Beautiful in what way?
(A) Oh, lots of white sand, different kinds of trees, you know.
(B) ___*I see ...*___ What's the weather like there?
(A) Most of the time it's really nice.
(B) _____. Sounds nice!

Now practice the conversation with a partner.

2. What do <u>you</u> think? Complete each sentence with your own opinion and give a reason.

Reason

- _____ is a sport I'd love to try. _____
- I think _____ is a beautiful place. _____
- I'd love to go to _____ someday. _____
- I think _____ is/are always a good gift. _____
- I thought "A Gift of Gold" was a/an _____ story. _____

3. *Pairs.* Share your opinions with a partner. Try to use the expressions above.

Example:
(A) Scuba diving is a sport I'd love to try.
(B) Really? Why scuba diving?
(A) _____

4. Sometimes people use the expressions below when they are <u>deciding how to answer a question</u>. Listen to the conversation below and write the missing expressions.

USEFUL EXPRESSIONS

Let me think.	It's hard to say.	Oh …
I'm not sure.	That's a hard question.	Uhmm …
It depends.	Good question.	Well …

(A) What are the most difficult sports you've tried?

(B) Uhmm … _____ _____ _____ … I guess I'd say skydiving and rock climbing.

(A) Interesting. Which one did you like better?

(B) _____ _____ _____ _____. Skydiving was probably more exciting but rock climbing was harder.

(A) Hmmm. I've gone rock climbing a few times, but I've never gone skydiving.

(B) Really? You should try it. It's a lot of fun.

5. Respond to the questions below. Write your answers on the lines. Use a useful expression from pages 59–60.

Example:
What's the most dangerous sport in the world?
 That's hard to say. It's probably car racing or skiing.

(A) What's the best program on TV?

(B) _____

(A) Do you look more like your mother or father?

(B) _____

(A) What can you do in Hawaii?

(B) _____

(A) Where's the best place to go on a date?

(B) _____

6. *Pairs.* Take turns asking the questions above. Expand your answers and ask more questions to keep your conversation going.

Topic: **Movies**
Language: **Describing**
Focus: **Relative clauses**

PRESENTATION

1. *Pairs.* Have you seen or heard of these movies? Tell your partner.

We asked the owner of a video store to suggest some good movies. Below are four of her suggestions.

Example:
I've seen the *Wizard of Oz.*
I've heard of the *Wizard of Oz,* but I've never seen it.
I've never heard of the *Wizard of Oz.*

E.T.: The Extra-Terrestrial

The Wizard of Oz

The African Queen

Ghost

2. *Pairs.* Use the photographs to complete the chart below.

Name of movie	What's it about?	Who's in it?	When was it made?
	It's about a dead man who returns to help his girlfriend.	Patrick Swayze Demi Moore	1990
	It's about four people who seek help from the Wizard of Oz—a girl who wants to go home, a Scarecrow who needs a brain, a Tin Man who wants a heart, and a Cowardly Lion who needs courage.	Judy Garland Ray Bolger Jack Haley Bert Lahr	1939
	It's about an alien who comes to Earth and becomes friends with a young boy.	Henry Thomas	1982
	It's about a man and a woman who travel down a river in Africa.	Katharine Hepburn Humphrey Bogart	1951

⏻ Listen and check your ideas.

PRACTICE

1. **Read the sentences in the box and answer the
   questions below.**

   DESCRIBING: *Relative clauses*

   a. In *Ghost*, Patrick Swayze stars as a ghost **who returns to help his girlfriend.**
   b. In *The African Queen*, Katharine Hepburn stars as a woman **who travels downriver in Africa.**
   c. *E.T.* is about an alien **who comes to Earth and becomes friends with a young boy.**
   d. A film buff is someone **that knows a lot about movies.**
   e. What do you call a movie **that makes you laugh?**
   f. A musical is a movie **that has singing and dancing.**
   g. I like movies **that have a lot of action.**

   - Circle the word *who* in the sentences. Underline the word <u>that</u>. When do we use *who*?
     When do we use *that*?
   - Look at sentences "f." and "g." One sentence uses *have*, the other uses *has*. Why?

   Answers on page 100

2. *Pairs.* **Make a guess. What do you think these films
   are about? Choose from the list on the right.**

   a. In *Roman Holiday*, Audrey Hepburn stars as a princess   • that eats swimmers.
   b. *Trouble in Paradise* is about two thieves   • that wants to be a dog.
   c. *Babe* is about a pig   • who runs away from home.
   d. *Twister* is about two scientists   • that has special powers.
   e. *Jaws* is about a huge shark   • who study dangerous tornados.
   f. In *The Mask*, Jim Carrey finds a mask   • who fall in and out of love.

   Compare ideas with another pair. Then listen and
   check your answers.

   Example:
   Ⓐ What's the movie *Roman Holiday* about?
   Ⓑ It's about a princess who runs away from home.

   PRONUNCIATION POINT: *Sentence intonation*

   ●   ●
   Babe is about a pig that wants to be a dog.
   Go to page 90.

3. **Talk to three classmates. Get answers to complete the chart.**

What's a good movie to see?	What's it about?
1 *Down by Law*	*It's about three men who escape from prison.*
2	
3	
4	

4. *Groups.* **Get together with your classmates and tell
   about the movies in your chart.**

   Example:
   Down by Law is a good movie to see. It's about three men who escape from prison.

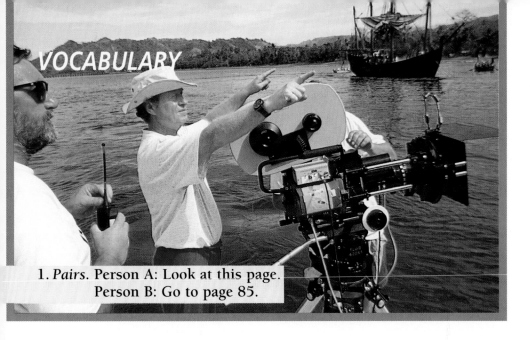

VOCABULARY

1. *Pairs*. Person A: Look at this page.
   Person B: Go to page 85.

2. Person A: Read the sentences under "Across."
   Add the <u>underlined</u> words to the puzzle.

ACROSS

1 A movie that tells a true story is called a <u>documentary</u>.
5 The person who writes the movie script is called a <u>screenwriter</u>.
8 A person who writes about movies for a newspaper is called a "movie <u>critic</u>."
11 The written words that appear with a foreign language film are called <u>subtitles</u>.
12 A movie that loses a lot of money is a <u>flop</u>.
13 A movie that is very scary is called a "<u>horror</u> film."

DOWN

2 A movie that makes you laugh is called a _____.
3 The list of names at the end of a film is called the _____.
4 The person who has the most important role in a film is called the _____.
5 Movies that take place in the future are called "_____ fiction films."
6 A movie that makes a lot of money is called a _____.
7 The person who directs the film is called the _____.
9 A movie that remains popular for a very long time is called a _____.
10 Someone who knows a lot about movies is called a "film _____."

3. Person A: Ask your partner questions. Add the answers to the puzzle.

   Example:
   Ⓐ What do you call a movie that makes you laugh?
   Ⓑ A comedy.
   Ⓐ How do you spell that?
   Ⓑ C-O-M-E-D-Y.
   Ⓐ Thanks.

What do you call...?

4. Person A: Now answer your partner's questions.

PREVIEW

1. What can you say when you like a film? What can you say when you <u>don't</u> like it? Listen and check (✓) the comments you hear.

Positive comments	Negative comments
☐ It wasn't bad.	☐ It didn't live up to expectations.
☐ It was a pleasant surprise.	☐ It was a disappointment.
☐ It was pretty good.	☐ It was pretty bad.
☐ It was great!	☐ It was awful!
☐ It was one of the best films I've ever seen!	☐ It was one of the worst films I've ever seen!

2. *Pairs.* Read these conversations. Do you think the missing words will be positive or negative?

(A) Have you seen *Independence Day*?
(B) Yes. On video.
(A) What did you think of it?
(B) I thought it was _____.
(A) Really? So it's worth seeing?
(B) Yes. Definitely.

(A) Have you seen *Nightmare on Elm Street*?
(B) Yes. I saw it a few years ago.
(A) What did you think of it?
(B) I thought it was _____.
(A) Really? So it's not worth seeing?
(B) I don't think so.

Now listen and complete the conversations. Then read the conversations out loud with your partner.

3. List three movies you want to see. Then find classmates who have seen these movies and get their opinions.

I want to see...
1.
2.
3.

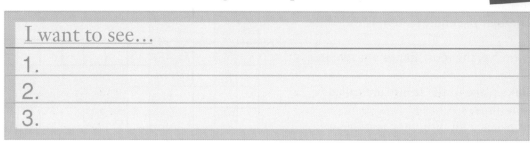

(A) Have you seen _____?

(B) Yes, _____.
(A) What did you think of it?
(B) _____.

(B) No, I haven't. Have you?
(A) No, but I'd like to.

Do you still want to see all three movies? Why or why not?

READ AND EVALUATE

1. Read the movie review below. Circle the positive comments. Underline the negative comments.

'Roses' Fails to Deliver

By Katie Connolly

"Bed of Roses" is a fairly good movie, but it did not live up to expectations. The previews and advertisements promised something more sophisticated and exciting, but the actors and writers tried too hard to make the movie emotional instead. It was too sappy,[1] not as romantic as I hoped it would be.

The movie is basically a love story that begins with a somewhat unbelievable situation. Christian Slater plays a florist who anonymously sends flowers[2] to a young woman, played by Mary Stuart Masterson. The flowers are meant to cheer her up,[3] because he saw her crying. The next morning he follows her to work and hands over the flowers; she thinks he's just the delivery man. Eventually he tells her the truth, they spend a day together, he sends her more flowers—and then they become a couple.

Later, things start to go wrong. Masterson is nervous about getting too serious, and Slater scares her off by proposing to her[4] in front of his family on Christmas.

Christian Slater is a good actor, but his character in this film seems too perfect. He is sweet, charming and romantic, but he is not realistic.

"Bed of Roses" is a nice innocent love story, but it fell short in delivering on romance and realism.[5] Only the ending was uplifting[6] and sincere.

Stars arrive at scene

Katie Connolly is a student at Archbishop Williams High School in Massachusetts. This review appeared in The Boston Globe.

---

[1] **sappy:** too sentimental
[2] **anonymously sends flowers:** sends flowers without giving his name
[3] **cheer her up:** make her happy
[4] **proposing to her:** asking her to marry him
[5] it **fell short in delivering on romance and realism:** it was neither romantic nor realistic
[6] **the ending was uplifting:** the ending was happy and positive

2. *Pairs.* Did you underline or circle the same words and phrases? Compare ideas.

SUMMARIZE

1. *Groups.* Work together to answer these questions about the movie review on page 65.

   a. What does this writer like about the movie? What does she dislike?
   b. Does this review make you want to see the movie? Why or why not?

   Report your group's answers to the class.

2. *Groups.* The movie review on page 65 has five paragraphs. In the chart below, check (✓) the information that you find in each paragraph.

	She evaluates the acting.	She gives her opinion of the movie.	She tells what the movie is about.	She identifies the movie.
Paragraph 1	☐	☐	☐	☐
Paragraph 2	☐	☐	☐	☐
Paragraph 3	☐	☐	☐	☐
Paragraph 4	☐	☐	☐	☐
Paragraph 5	☐	☐	☐	☐

SHARE INFORMATION

1. *Pairs.* Choose a movie that you have both seen. Work together to answer these questions. Take notes in the chart.

A movie we've both seen:	
a. What's it about?	
b. Who's in the movie? What's your opinion of the acting?	
c. Is it worth seeing? Why or why not?	

2. Talk to different classmates. Ask each person about the movie they chose.

3. What movies did you hear about? Tell the class.

Topic: **Health**
Language: **Identifying possible consequences**
Focus: **If clauses with modals: will, might**

PRESENTATION

1. *Pairs.* Do you think these statements are true or false?
   Check (✓) your answers.

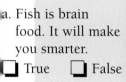

a. Fish is brain
food. It will make
you smarter.
☐ True   ☐ False

b. If you wear garlic around your neck,
you won't catch a cold.
☐ True   ☐ False

c. If you cross your
eyes, they might
stay that way.
☐ True   ☐ False

d. Listening to loud music might damage your hearing.
☐ True   ☐ False

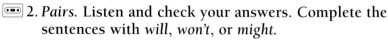

🔲 2. *Pairs.* **Listen and check your answers. Complete the
sentences with *will*, *won't*, or *might*.**

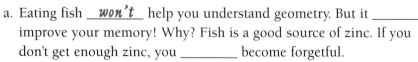

a. Eating fish __*won't*__ help you understand geometry. But it _____
improve your memory! Why? Fish is a good source of zinc. If you
don't get enough zinc, you _____ become forgetful.

b. Wearing garlic around your neck _____ keep you healthy. But eating garlic _____!
Microbiologist James North found that garlic actually kills some kinds of bacteria.

c. "Don't worry. You can cross your eyes as much as you want,
and they _____ stay that way," says eye doctor Richard Silver.

d. If you listen to loud music for long periods of time, you _____
damage your hearing. That's why some rock musicians wear earplugs at concerts.

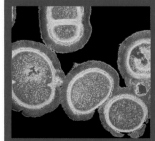

PRACTICE

1. Read the *if* clauses and check (✓) the possible consequences.

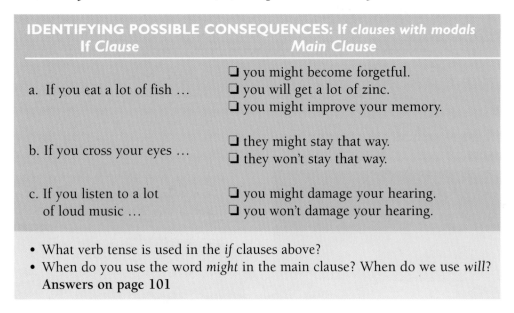

IDENTIFYING POSSIBLE CONSEQUENCES: If *clauses with modals*	
If Clause	*Main Clause*
a. If you eat a lot of fish …	❏ you might become forgetful. ❏ you will get a lot of zinc. ❏ you might improve your memory.
b. If you cross your eyes …	❏ they might stay that way. ❏ they won't stay that way.
c. If you listen to a lot of loud music …	❏ you might damage your hearing. ❏ you won't damage your hearing.

• What verb tense is used in the *if* clauses above?
• When do you use the word *might* in the main clause? When do we use *will*?
  Answers on page 101

2. Complete each sentence with a possible consequence.
   (More than one answer is possible.)

   a. If you don't drink water for several days,
   b. If you eat a lot of chocolate,
   c. If you drink a lot of coffee,
   d. If you eat a lot of fruits and vegetables,
   e. If you exercise regularly,
   f. If you don't wear a coat in the winter,
   g. If you quit smoking,

POSSIBLE CONSEQUENCES

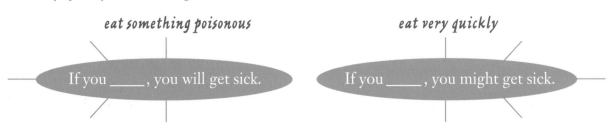

you'll feel better.
you'll die.
you'll feel more awake.

you might get sick.
you might live longer.
you might gain weight.

you won't be able to sleep at night.
you won't feel well.
you won't feel tired in the morning.

3. *Pairs*. Compare answers with a classmate.

4. *Groups*. Add each idea to a diagram below. Then add
   your own ideas.

   • eat something poisonous • go without food for several weeks
   • eat very quickly   • go outside without a coat in the winter

eat something poisonous   *eat very quickly*

If you _____, you will get sick.   If you _____, you might get sick.

Read your group's ideas to the class.

WHAT DO YOU THINK?

1. *Pairs.* What are the possible consequences of each action in the chart? Choose from the list below.

you might damage your heart   you might damage your skin
you might get skin cancer   you might get lung cancer
your bones and muscles will get stronger   you won't get fat

	Possible Consequences
a. If you spend a lot of time in the sun,	*you might damage your skin.*
b. If you exercise regularly,	
c. If you smoke cigarettes,	

Can you think of any more consequences?
Add them to the chart.

2. Report to the class.

PRONUNCIATION POINT: *Reduced forms*
/yəmaɪt/
If you smoke, you might get cancer.
Go to page 90.

SURVEY

1. Find two people who answer *Yes* to each question. Then find out the reason for their answers.

Example:
Ⓐ Do you think it's unhealthy to spend a lot of time in the sun?
Ⓑ Yes, I do.
Ⓐ Why is that?
Ⓑ You might get skin cancer.

Do you think it's ...?	Names	Reasons
unhealthy to sit in the sun all day		
important to exercise regularly		
unhealthy to smoke cigarettes		

2. Report to the class.

PREVIEW

1. *Pairs.* Look at this graph and read the sentences below. Check (✓) *That's true* or *That's false.*

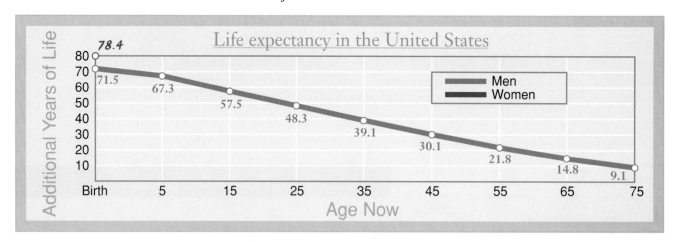

	That's true.	That's false.
a. At birth, a man in the U.S. can expect to live for 71.5 years.	❏	❏
b. If you are a 25-year-old man, you can expect to live for 39.1 years more.	❏	❏
c. A man who is 75 years old can expect to live for 9.1 more years.	❏	❏

2. What is the life expectancy of a woman in the U.S.?
Listen and add the information to the graph.

3. *Pairs.* Which of these activities below might lengthen your life?
Which might shorten it? Write *L* for lengthen or *S* for shorten.

___ living in an urban area (a city)   ___ being married

___ living alone   ___ smoking

___ working behind a desk   ___ getting a college education

___ sunbathing   ___ earning a high salary

Compare ideas with another pair.

Example:
(A) We think living in a city might shorten your life.
(B) Why do you think so?
(A) Because the air is dirty and it might make you sick.

READ AND RESPOND

1. *Pairs.* Ask your partner the questions on page 71.
Calculate your partner's life expectancy.

2. *Groups.* According to the survey, which activities will
lengthen your life? Which activities will shorten
your life? List your ideas.

HOW TO CALCULATE YOUR LIFE EXPECTANCY

A *Start with the number 74*   **74** _____

B *Gender*

1. Are you male? If yes, subtract 3. Are you female? Add 4. _____

> That's right. There's a seven-year difference between the sexes.

C *Lifestyle*

2. Do you live in an urban area with a population over 2 million? Subtract 2. Do you live in a town with a population under 10,000 or on a farm? Add 2. _____

> Living in a city is bad for your health. There's too much pollution and tension!

3. Do you work or expect to work behind a desk? Subtract 3. Does your work require regular, heavy physical labor? Add 3. _____

4. Do you exercise strenuously (tennis, running, swimming, etc.) five times a week for at least a half-hour? Add 2. _____

5. Do you live with a spouse, relative or friend? Add 5. If not, subtract 1 for every 10 years alone since age 25. _____

> People together eat better, take care of each other, and are less depressed.

D *Personality*

6. Do you sleep more than 10 hours each night? If so, subtract 4. _____

7. Are you intense, aggressive, easily angered? Subtract 3. Are you easygoing, relaxed, a follower? Add 3. _____

8. Are you happy? Add 1. Unhappy? Subtract 2. _____

E *Success*

9. Are you or do you expect to be rich? If so, subtract 2. _____

> Having a lot of money might lead to high living and tension.

10. Did you finish college? Add 2. Do you expect to finish college? Add 2. Do you have a graduate degree? Add 2 more. _____

> People with higher education seem to live more sensibly— at least that's the theory.

11. Do you plan to work after the age of 65? Add 3. _____

> That's right. Retirement kills.

F *Health*

12. Do you smoke more than two packs of cigarettes a day? Subtract 8. One to two packs a day? Subtract 6. One half to one? Subtract 3. _____

13. Are you overweight by 22.5 kg or more? Subtract 8. By 13.5 to 22.5 kg? Subtract 4. By 4.5 kg to 13.5 kg? Subtract 2. _____

G *Age Adjustment*

14. Are you between 30 and 40? Add 2. Between 40 and 50? Add 3. Between 50 and 70? Add 4. _____

COLLECT INFORMATION

1. Who is the oldest person you know well? Think about this person and take notes in the chart below.

Example:

The Oldest Person I Know

Relationship _____
Age _____ Gender _____
Lifestyle _____

Personality _____

Success _____

Health _____

The Oldest Person I Know

Relationship My great-grandmother
Age 94 Gender female
Lifestyle She lives in a small town. She worked for many years as a nursery school teacher. She never worked behind a desk. She didn't play any sports regularly, but she always liked to walk a lot.

Personality She's not aggressive or easily angered. She's easygoing and happy.

Success She wasn't rich. She has a graduate degree.

Health She smoked a little when she was young, but she quit smoking when she was in her 30s.

2. *Groups.* Take turns telling about the person in your chart.

3. *Groups.* Look for similarities among the oldest people you know. Based on this information, what might help you to live a long life? List five ideas.

Example:
You might live longer if you live in a small town.
All of the oldest people we know are female, so if you're female you might live longer.

Topic: **Plans and goals**
Language: **Talking about future plans**
Focus: Be going to; present continuous

PRESENTATION

1. *Pairs.* **What do you remember about these people?**

   Example:
   Ⓐ Amanda Block is the person who works at MTV. Right?
   Ⓑ Right. And she drinks a lot of coffee.

c. Mr. Park

a. Amanda Block

b. Sue Mattison

d. Greg Sergi

2. We asked these people about their future plans.
   Match each person to a plan below.

   ☐ She is planning to work at the Trois Vallees ski area in France next year.
   It is the largest ski area in the world.

   ☐ Because he is very poor now, he is going to work for one of his friends.
   Someday he hopes to buy some land and build a house.

   ☐ He plans to study a lot and spend a lot of time in the library. After college,
   he hopes to get a job in international business.

   ☐ She wants to be a producer at MTV. She would like to produce special
   programs about new rock bands.

3. *Pairs.* **Which person's plans sound the most
   interesting to you? Why?**

PRACTICE

1. What are <u>your</u> future plans? Read the sentences in the box and check (✓) *Yes* or *No*.

Talking About Future Plans: Be going to; *present continuous*

	YES	NO
a. **I'm going to** go overseas next year.	☐	☐
b. **I'm going** (to go) away next summer.	☐	☐
c. **I plan to** go to this school next year.	☐	☐
d. **I'm planning** to get a job/change jobs next year.	☐	☐
e. **I'm meeting** some friends after class.	☐	☐
f. **I'm studying** at home tonight.	☐	☐

- What verb tenses can you use to identify a future plan?

Answers on page 102

---

2. **Listen and complete the conversations.**

a. Yoko: What are you planning to do this summer?

   Ted: This summer? _____.

   Yoko: Really? What are you going to do there?

   Ted: _____.

   Yoko: Sounds interesting.

🔊 PRONUNCIATION POINT: *Reduced forms*
/gʊɪŋtə/
What are you going to do tonight?
Go to page 90.

b. Shirin: What do you plan to do this summer?

   Andy: _____. I'd like to travel, but I might have to work.

   Shirin: Hmm. Where would you like to go?

   Andy: _____. Someplace warm.

c. Maya: What are you going to do when you finish this course?

   Nick: Me? _____.

   Maya: Really? Have you started looking for one?

   Nick: _____.

Which person has definite plans?

LISTENING

1. *Pairs.* Put the lines of this conversation in order.

Person A

___ No, never. Is it nice?

___ Thanks, but I'm going to visit my grandparents.

_**1**_ Do you have any plans for the weekend?

___ So, how are you going to get there?

___ Really? Which beach?

Person B

___ Crescent Beach. Have you ever been there?

___ Very. It's a great place to swim.

___ We're going to drive. Hey, do you want to come with us? There's plenty of room.

_**2**_ Yeah. I'm going to the beach with a couple of friends.

🔊 Now listen and check your answers.

🔊 2. Listen to these people. Do they have plans for the weekend? Check (✓) *Yes* or *No*.

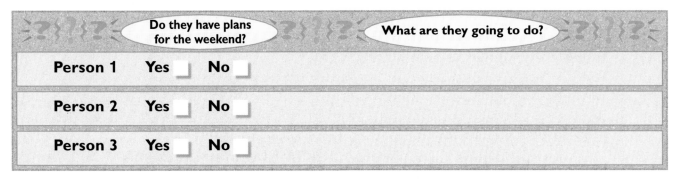

	Do they have plans for the weekend?	What are they going to do?
Person 1	Yes ☐ No ☐	
Person 2	Yes ☐ No ☐	
Person 3	Yes ☐ No ☐	

Now listen again and write two details about each person's plans.

GET THE DETAILS

1. Find out about your classmates' plans for this weekend. Ask questions to get more details.

Example:
Ⓐ Do you have plans for the weekend?
Ⓑ Yes. I'm going to visit my grandparents.
Ⓐ Oh? Do they live nearby?
Ⓑ _____

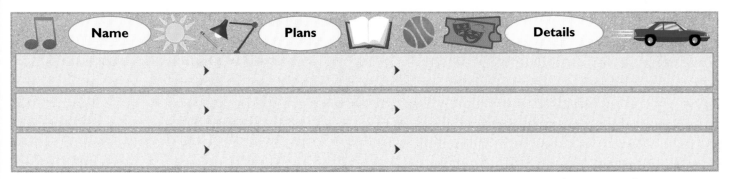

Name	Plans	Details
▸	▸	
▸	▸	
▸	▸	

2. Report to the class.

PREVIEW

1. *Pairs.* A goal is something you want to do in the
   future. Read this list of goals and check (✓) the
   things you want to do.

> I'd like to … I want to …
> I hope to … I intend to …

❏ buy a car
❏ buy a house
❏ be a good parent
❏ live a long, healthy life
❏ get rich
❏ be successful in my career
❏ retire when I'm 40

❏ have my own business
❏ learn another language
❏ meet people from other countries
❏ travel a lot
❏ become a teacher
❏ become a _____
❏ _____

2. *Pairs.* If you really want to reach your goals, it helps
   to make a plan. Match these goals and plans.
   (**More than one answer is possible.**)

Goals	Plans (What are you going to do to reach your goal?)
"I hope to live a long, healthy life." _____	a. "I plan to study in France."
	b. "I'm going to learn to play golf."
"I'd like to be successful in my career." _____	c. "I'm going to start saving money."
	d. "I'm going to eat well."
"I intend to have my own business." _____	e. "I'm going to get plenty of exercise."
	f. "I'm going to work hard."
"I want to learn another language." _____	g. "I plan to take some business courses."

READ AND TAKE NOTES ▭

1. Both of these people had a goal. Read the
   information on page 77 and complete the chart.

Name	Goal	What did they do to reach their goal?
Oscar Mendoza		*worked in a restaurant to earn money*
Anna Stebbins		

Oscar Mendoza

One thing I really wanted to do after high school was to travel around the United States. But you need money to travel and of course I didn't have any! I didn't want to ask my parents for help, so I got a job in a restaurant. I worked long hours—ten hours a day. But in two months I had enough money for my trip.

I didn't want to travel alone, so I asked my friend A.J. to come along. A.J. loves the outdoors—mountains, hiking, and things like that—so he wanted to camp out and visit the scenic spots. I'm interested in engineering and architecture, so I wanted to see the big cities like Chicago, Los Angeles, and Seattle. We weren't perfect traveling companions, but we decided to go together anyway.

Before we left, we spent a lot of time reading about places in the United States. I chose five places I really wanted to see and A.J. did too. That's how we planned our trip across the country.

Anna Stebbins

When I was a child, I had friends from several different countries. They could all speak two languages; some of them could speak three. That's probably why one of my goals was to learn to speak another language fluently.

After I graduated from high school, I enrolled in a university for foreign students in Florence, Italy. I didn't speak a word of Italian, but I figured that going there was the best way to learn.

At the university, I took Italian language courses for six hours a day, five days a week. I avoided other English-speaking people. I studied hard and practiced speaking Italian whenever I could. But it was horrible. My head hurt all the time and I felt like a five-year-old child because I couldn't talk about anything interesting or important. Then, after about six months, I realized that I was speaking Italian without thinking about it. I wasn't translating. I was thinking in Italian. That's when I knew I had done it.

2. *Groups.* Compare charts. Then answer the questions below.

   a. Do you think it's important to have goals? Why or why not?
   b. Do you think it's okay to change your goals? Give an example.

SHARE IDEAS

1. *Groups.* What do you think these people should do to reach their goals. Choose two people and list your group's suggestions.

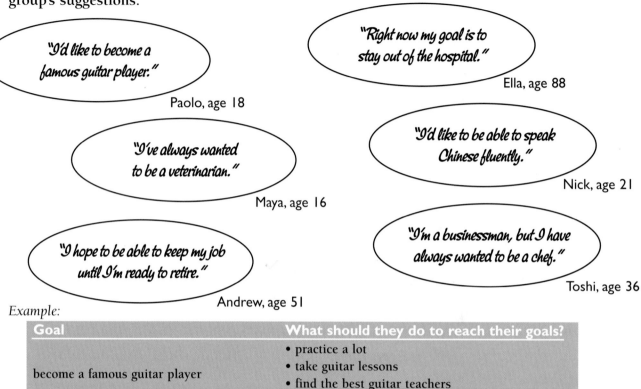

"I'd like to become a famous guitar player."

Paolo, age 18

"Right now my goal is to stay out of the hospital."

Ella, age 88

"I've always wanted to be a veterinarian."

Maya, age 16

"I'd like to be able to speak Chinese fluently."

Nick, age 21

"I hope to be able to keep my job until I'm ready to retire."

Andrew, age 51

"I'm a businessman, but I have always wanted to be a chef."

Toshi, age 36

Example:

Goal	What should they do to reach their goals?
become a famous guitar player	• practice a lot • take guitar lessons • find the best guitar teachers • listen to famous guitar players

2. Report your group's ideas to the class.

INTERVIEW

1. Identify one of your future goals. What are you going to do to reach this goal? Make a plan.

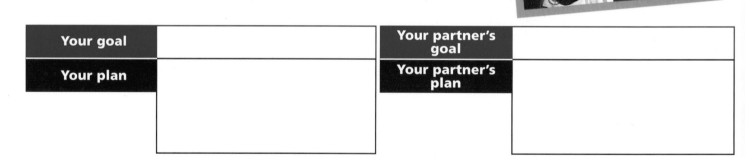

Your goal	
Your plan	

Your partner's goal	
Your partner's plan	

2. *Pairs.* Find out about your partner's goal. Then ask questions to get more information.

3. *Groups.* Tell the other people in your group about your partner's goal.

Unit 1

SHARE INFORMATION

Some verbs with irregular past tenses

drink	→ drank		meet	→ met
eat	→ ate		see	→ saw
get	→ got		take	→ took
go	→ went		wake up	→ woke up
have	→ had			

1. **What did <u>you</u> do yesterday? List seven things and the time of day you did them.**

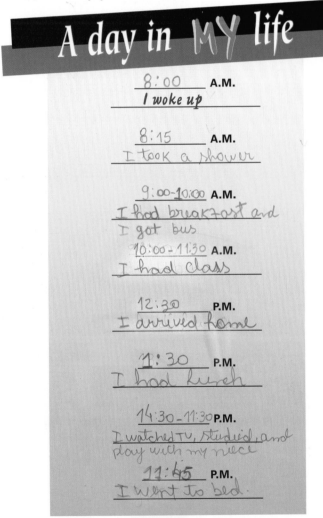

A day in MY life

8:00	A.M.
I woke up	

8:15	A.M.
I took a shower	

9:00–10:00	A.M.
I had breakfast and I got bus	

10:00–11:30	A.M.
I had class	

12:30	P.M.
I arrived home	

1:30	P.M.
I had lunch	

14:30–11:30	P.M.
I watched TV, studied, and play with my niece	

11:45	P.M.
I went to bed.	

Eliane

6:30 – I woke up
7:00 – I went to the gym
8:10 – I came back home
8:15 – I ate breakfast
8:35 – I took a shower
8:50 – I blew dry my hair and got dressed
9:00 – I taught English to Cleo
11:00 – I cooked lunch
12:00 – I had lunch
1:30 – I had painting class
4:30 – I arrived home
5:00 – I watched TV
6:00 – I had dinner
10:30 – I went to bed.

2. *Pairs.* Exchange schedules. Write five questions about your partner's schedule.

3. *Pairs.* Take turns asking and answering questions.

Unit 2

PERSON B'S PAGE

PREVIEW

2. **What do these people do at work? Use the chart to answer your partner's questions.**

Example:
Ⓐ Does Aaron Chang spend a lot of time outdoors?
Ⓑ Yes, he does.

What do these people do at work?

	Aaron Chang Yes	Aaron Chang No	Julie Krone Yes	Julie Krone No	Jack Horner Yes	Jack Horner No
spends a lot of time outdoors	✓		✓		✓	
often travels to foreign countries	✓			✓	✓	
gets up early to go to work		✓	✓		✓	
uses a camera at work	✓			✓	✓	
sometimes lives in a tent		✓		✓	✓	
uses a notebook and pen at work	✓			✓	✓	
works with animals		✓	✓		✓	
often works barefoot	✓			✓		✓
often needs to make quick decisions	✓		✓			✓
needs to be in good shape		✓	✓			✓
needs to wear special clothes at work		✓	✓			✓

3. **Now ask your partner questions to complete the chart.**

4. *Pairs.* **Can you guess each person's job?**

Example:
Ⓐ I think Julie Krone is a/an …
Ⓑ Why is that?
Ⓐ Because she …

photographer

architect

police officer

jockey

scientist

PERSON B'S PAGE

SHARE INFORMATION

2. Use the chart to answer your partner's questions.

   Example:
   (A) In the U.S., is it okay to put your feet up on the furniture?
   (B) Yes, it is.
   (A) How about in Ecuador? Is it okay to put your feet up there?

IS IT OKAY...	The U.S.		China		Ecuador	
	Yes	No	Yes	No	Yes	No
a. ...to put your feet up on the furniture?	✓			✓		✓
b. ...to arrive early for a party?		✓		✓	✓	
c. ...to ask "How much money do you make?"		✓	✓			✓
d. ...to ask a woman "How old are you?"		✓	✓			✗
e. ...to use a toothpick in a restaurant?		✓	✓			✓
f. ...to use a cellular phone in a restaurant?		✓	✓		✓	
g. ...to call a teacher by his/her first name?	✓			✓		✓
h. ...to talk to your teacher with your hands in your pockets?	✓			✓		✓

3. Now ask your partner questions to complete the chart.

4. *Pairs.* How are customs similar and different in these countries? Write three ideas.

   Example:
   In the U.S., it's okay to put your feet up on the furniture, but it's not okay in China.

VOCABULARY

2. Read the sentences under "Down." Add the underlined words to the puzzle.

DOWN

1 People sometimes carry <u>umbrellas</u> to protect themselves from the rain.
2 You can wear <u>boots</u> to keep your feet warm and dry in the mud.
3 Motorcyclists wear <u>helmets</u> to protect their heads.
5 <u>Sandals</u> are popular footwear in hot weather.
6 Another word for women's pants is <u>slacks</u>.
7 A traditional Japanese robe is called a <u>kimono</u>.

ACROSS

4 What do you call the shoes people wear indoors?
5 What do you call a dress without sleeves? SLiPPE (Answer: a _____ dress) SLEEVELESS
8 What's another name for wooden shoes? CLOGS
9 What do you call the pants and shirt a person sleeps in? PAJAMAS
10 What can women wear to cover their hair? SCAR
11 What do people wear on their hands to keep them warm? GLOVES

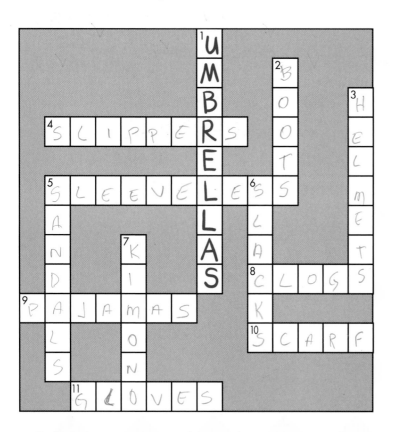

3. **Answer your partner's questions.**

Example:
Ⓐ What can people carry to protect themselves from the rain?
Ⓑ Umbrellas.
Ⓐ How do you spell that?
Ⓑ U-M-B-R-E-L-L-A-S.
Ⓐ Thanks.

4. **Now ask your partner the questions under "Across."**
   Add the answers to your puzzle.

PERSON B'S PAGE

READ AND COMPARE

2. Read about this unusual car and answer the questions in the chart.

The Lean Machine

Jerry Williams and a team of four people wanted to build a one-person car that was more fuel efficient than an ordinary car. The team worked for eight years to design the Lean Machine. This unusual car can go 68.2 miles per hour (110 km/h). It only needs 1 gallon (4 liters) of gasoline to travel 720 miles (1,161 km). The designers named it the Lean Machine because the passenger section of the car tilts. This prevents the car from skidding or turning over when it goes around a sharp turn. The motor section of the car does not tilt. It always remains upright.

	The Lean Machine	The Aircar
How big is it?	It's smaller than an ordinary car.	It has a greater...
How fast can it go?	it can go 110 Kmh	
How many people can it hold?	it can hold one-person	
How is it different from an ordinary car?		

3. Answer your partner's questions about the Lean Machine.

4. Now ask your partner questions about the Aircar to complete the chart above.

5. *Pairs.* Use your chart to answer these questions.

   a. Which car is faster?
   b. Which car is more useful?
   c. Which car is larger?
   d. Which car is more fuel efficient?
   e. Which car would you rather buy? Why?

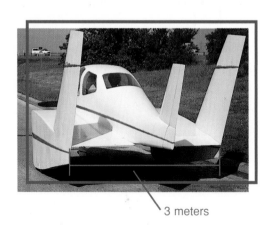

3 meters

GUESS THE ENDING!

3. Read the end of the story.

... continued from page 57

A Gift of Gold *(part 2)*

"This ox looks like a fine animal. And it's very large," said the King when his secretary brought Mr. Park's gift to him. "I shall give the man who brought it a gift. What have I received recently that I can give him?"

"Well, Your Majesty, there is that enormous persimmon you received a few days ago," replied his secretary.

"Oh, yes. That will do nicely," said the King.

Mr. Park fainted when the King's secretary presented him with the persimmon. And that is how he became a poor man.

4. *Groups*. Answer the questions below, then report to the class.

a. Did you like the story? Why or why not?

b. The purpose of some folktales is to teach people how to behave. What do you think the folktale is trying to teach?

VOCABULARY

2. Read the sentences under "Down." Add the underlined words to the puzzle.

DOWN

2 A movie that makes you laugh is called a <u>comedy</u>.

3 The list of names at the end of a film is called the <u>credits</u>.

4 The person who has the most important role in a film is called the <u>star</u>.

5 Movies that take place in the future are called "<u>science</u> fiction films."

6 A movie that makes a lot of money is called a <u>blockbuster</u>.

7 The person who directs the film is called the <u>director</u>.

9 A movie that remains popular for a very long time is called a <u>classic</u>.

10 Someone who knows a lot about movies is called a "film <u>buff</u>."

ACROSS

1 A movie that tells a true story is called a _____.

5 The person who writes the movie script is called a _____.

8 A person who writes about movies for a newspaper is called a "movie _____."

11 The written words that appear with a foreign language film are called _____.

12 A movie that loses a lot of money is a _____.

13 A movie that is very scary is called a "_____ film."

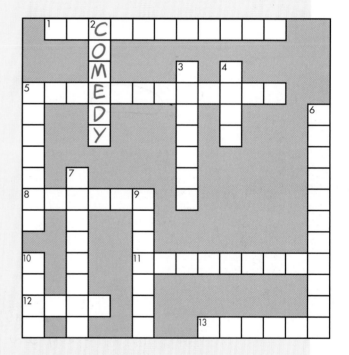

3. Answer your partner's questions.

Example:
Ⓐ What do you call a movie that makes you laugh?
Ⓑ A comedy.
Ⓐ How do you spell that?
Ⓑ C-o-m-e-d-y.
Ⓐ Thanks.

4. Ask your partner questions to complete the puzzle.

What do you call...?

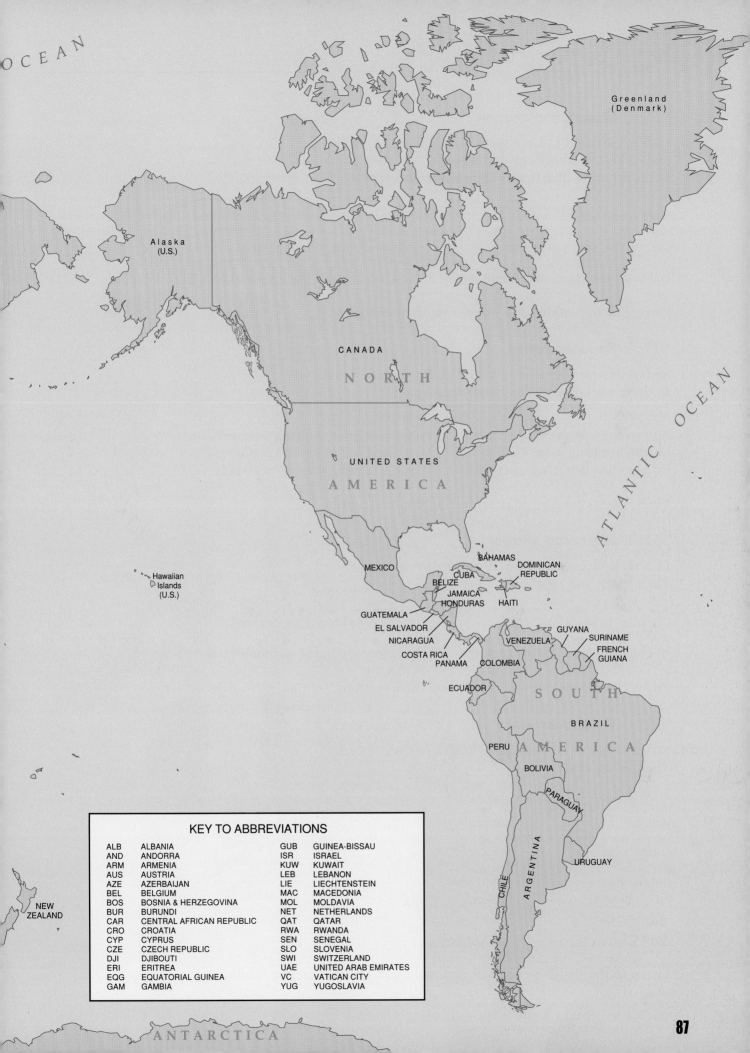

OCEAN

Greenland
(Denmark)

Alaska
(U.S.)

CANADA

N O R T H

UNITED STATES

A M E R I C A

ATLANTIC OCEAN

Hawaiian
Islands
(U.S.)

MEXICO

BAHAMAS

CUBA   DOMINICAN
              REPUBLIC
BELIZE
JAMAICA
HONDURAS   HAITI
GUATEMALA

EL SALVADOR   GUYANA
NICARAGUA   VENEZUELA   SURINAME
                               FRENCH
COSTA RICA   GUIANA
PANAMA   COLOMBIA

ECUADOR   S O U T H

                 A M E R I C A

BRAZIL

PERU

BOLIVIA

PARAGUAY

NEW
ZEALAND

CHILE   ARGENTINA

URUGUAY

KEY TO ABBREVIATIONS

ALB	ALBANIA	GUB	GUINEA-BISSAU
AND	ANDORRA	ISR	ISRAEL
ARM	ARMENIA	KUW	KUWAIT
AUS	AUSTRIA	LEB	LEBANON
AZE	AZERBAIJAN	LIE	LIECHTENSTEIN
BEL	BELGIUM	MAC	MACEDONIA
BOS	BOSNIA & HERZEGOVINA	MOL	MOLDAVIA
BUR	BURUNDI	NET	NETHERLANDS
CAR	CENTRAL AFRICAN REPUBLIC	QAT	QATAR
CRO	CROATIA	RWA	RWANDA
CYP	CYPRUS	SEN	SENEGAL
CZE	CZECH REPUBLIC	SLO	SLOVENIA
DJI	DJIBOUTI	SWI	SWITZERLAND
ERI	ERITREA	UAE	UNITED ARAB EMIRATES
EQG	EQUATORIAL GUINEA	VC	VATICAN CITY
GAM	GAMBIA	YUG	YUGOSLAVIA

A N T A R C T I C A

PRONUNCIATION POINTS

UNIT 1: Question intonation

1. Listen. Notice that your voice goes up (___↗) at the
end of Yes/No questions and down (___↘) at the end
of information questions. Then listen and repeat.

Does Amanda Block work?

Do you live with your parents?

Did you have breakfast this morning?

When did Amanda Block have lunch?

How do you get home from school?

What time did you get up today?

2. *Pairs.* Practice asking and answering the questions.

UNIT 2: Reduced forms

1. Listen. Notice the pronunciation of *Do you* and *Would you*
in these questions. Then listen and repeat.

/dəyə/

Do you enjoy studying English?
Do you like living here?
Do you mind doing homework?

/wʊdʒə/

Would you enjoy studying German?
Would you like to live in London?
Would you mind walking to school?

2. *Pairs.* Practice asking and answering the questions.

UNIT 3: Sentence stress

1. Listen. Notice the rhythm of these questions.
Then listen and repeat.

Is it okay to smoke in a taxi?

Is it okay to shout in a restaurant?

Is it okay to chew gum in class?

Is it okay to point at someone?

2. *Pairs.* Practice asking and answering the questions.

UNIT 4: Syllable stress

1. Listen. Notice the stressed syllables in these words.
Then listen and repeat.

1st syllable	2nd syllable
● · ·	· ● ·
popular	expensive
● · ·	· ● ·
comfortable	important
● · ·	· ● ·
interesting	traditional

a. fashionable
b. uncomfortable
c. unpopular
d. dangerous
e. official
f. practical

2. Listen to the words in the box and add them to the correct column.

UNIT 5: Sentence stress

Listen. Notice the stressed words in these responses.
Then listen and repeat.

A I like this music.

● · ●
B So do I.

● · ●
I do too.

● ●
Me too.

A I don't really like this music.

● · · ●
B Neither do I.

● · ● ·
I don't either.

● ● ·
Me neither.

UNIT 6: Questions of choice

1. Listen. Notice the intonation in these questions of choice. Then listen and repeat.

Would you rather have a big car or a small car?

Would you rather rent a video or go to the movies?

Would you rather buy a CD or a cassette?

Would you rather fax a letter or mail it?

2. *Pairs.* Practice asking and answering the questions.

UNIT 7: Unstressed words

1. Listen and write the number of words you hear in each question. Then listen again and write the questions.

a. _5_ *Have you ever played volleyball?*
b. ____ What did you do an your last vacation?
c. ____ Have you even gone snorkiling?
d. ____ What is your favorite sport?
e. ____ Do you like to watch sport on Tv?

2. *Pairs.* Practice asking and answering the questions.

UNIT 8: Sentence stress

1. Listen. Notice how we stress the most important words in a sentence. Then listen and repeat.

●   ●   ●   ●
Bali is one of the most beautiful places in the world.

       ●   ●   ●   ●   ●
The Colosseum is one of the most popular tourist spots in Rome.

2. Fill in the blanks with names of places you know. Then practice saying the sentences.

Bali is one of the most beautiful places in _the world_

The colosseum is one of the most popular tourist spots in _Rome_.

UNIT 9: Final -s

🔊 1. Listen. Notice the pronunciation of the final -s.

/s/	/z/	/ɪz/
books	flowers	watches

🔊 2. Listen and check (✓) the correct column
for each word.

	/s/	/z/	/ɪz/
a. birthday presents	☐	☐	☐
b. birthday cards	☐	☐	☐
c. CDs	☐	☐	☐
d. boxes of candy	☐	☐	☐
e. T-shirts	☐	☐	☐
f. videos	☐	☐	☐
g. concert tickets	☐	☐	☐

UNIT 10: Sentence stress

🔊 Listen. Notice the intonation of these sentences.
Then listen and repeat.

Babe is about a pig that wants to be a dog.

Independence Day is about aliens that attack Earth.

King Kong is about a giant ape that climbs the Empire State Building.

Jurassic Park is about dinosaurs that come back to life.

UNIT 11: Reduced forms

🔊 Listen. Notice the pronunciation of *you* in these
sentences. Then listen and repeat.

/yəmaɪt/
If you smoke, you might get cancer.

/yəl/
If you eat a lot of chocolate, you'll get fat.

/yəwoʊnt/
If you drink coffee at night, you won't sleep well.

UNIT 12: Reduced forms

🔊 1. Listen. Notice the pronunciation of *going to*.
Then listen and repeat.

/goʊɪŋtə/
What are you going to do tonight?
What are you going to do this summer?
What are you going to do when you finish this course?

2. *Pairs.* Practice asking and answering the questions.

Grammar Guide

UNIT 1: *Questions with* do *and* did

> **Answers from page 2**
> • **Which questions ask something about the past? Which words help you to know?**
> Questions "b." and "e." ask about the past. The words *did, last year,* and *the next morning* help you to know.
> • **Which questions ask for a *yes* or *no* answer? How do you know?**
> You can answer questions "a." and "b." with *yes* or *no.* When a question begins with *do, does,* or *did,* you can answer with *yes* or *no.*

TIPS ON FORM AND USAGE

(1)

	Examples		Explanations

Do I / you / we / they **get up** early? **study** English?
Does he / she / it

Use *do* or *does* + the simple form of the verb to ask about habits or the general present.

> A list of irregular verbs appears on page 103.

(2)
• **Did** you **stay up** late last night?
• **Did** she **call** last night?

Use *did* + the simple form of the verb to ask questions about the past.

(3)
• **Do** you live here? *(Yes, I do.)*
• **Did** they go anywhere last night? *(No, they didn't.)*
• **Where** do you live? *(In Tokyo.)*
• **Where** did you go last? *(To the movies.)*

If you begin your question with *do, does,* or *did,* you will get a *yes* or *no* answer. If you want more information than *yes* or *no,* use a *wh-* word *(who, what, where, when, why, which)* in your question.

1. **Which questions would you answer with *yes* or *no?* Check (✓) them.**

   - ❏ a. When do you usually get up?
   - ☒ b. Did you watch TV last night?
   - ❏ c. Where do you usually eat dinner?
   - ☒ d. Do you have a lot of friends?
   - ❏ e. Why did you leave so early yesterday?

2. **Find and correct the mistakes in these questions. (Some questions may be correct.)**

   a. How many hours a week does your teacher ~~works~~? *work*
   b. When did you first ~~studies~~ English? *study*
   c. When did you ~~met~~ your best friend? *meet*
   d. Why ~~do~~ it always rain on the weekend? *does*
   e. Did you have breakfast this morning?
   f. ~~Do~~ you stay up late last night? *DID?*

UNIT 2: *Verb + infinitive/gerund*

Answers from page 8
- Which verbs appear in both groups?
like, hate, love

YOU CAN USE A GERUND AFTER THESE VERBS:			
dislike *ing*	finish	miss *perder*	recommend
enjoy	give up	practice	spend time *pasar*
feel like	mind	quit *x deixar parar desaupan desistir*	suggest

Example: *I dislike getting up early in the morning.*

YOU CAN USE AN INFINITIVE AFTER THESE VERBS:			
afford *to*	choose	intend	refuse
agree *to*	decide	learn *to*	want *to* *wanna*
ask *to*	expect	need	would like
	hope	promise	

Example: *I can't afford to buy a Mercedes Benz.*

YOU CAN USE A GERUND OR AN INFINITIVE AFTER THESE VERBS:		
begin	hate	prefer
can't stand	like	start
continue	love	try

Example: They began eating at 1:00./They began to eat at 1:00.

Make sentences

---

1. **Complete each question with a correct form of the verb in parentheses.**

   a. How old were you when you learned _to walk_? (*walk*)
   b. What do you want _to learn_ in your English class? (*learn*) OK
   c. What do you feel like _doing_ this weekend? (*do*)
   d. Would you mind _living_ on a boat? (*live*)
   e. How much time do you usually spend _sleeping_? (*sleep*)

2. **Answer each question above. Use a complete sentence.**

   a. I was 2 years old when I learned to walk.
   b. I want to learn to speak English very well.
   c. I feel like visiting my friend Aida.
   d. Yes, I would. Because I'm afraid of water.
   e. I usually spend 8 hours sleeping

UNIT 3: It's + adjective + infinitive; gerunds as subjects

TIPS ON FORM AND USAGE: It's + adjective + infinitive

Examples	Explanations
1 • **It's** important to be on time for a business meeting. • In Japan, **it's** rude to blow your nose in public.	You can use *it's* + an adjective + an infinitive to give an opinion.
2 • **It's** not rude to eat a sandwich with your fingers. (= *It's okay to eat a sandwich with your fingers.*) • It's rude **not** to use a spoon when you eat soup. (= *It's important to use a spoon when you eat soup.*)	You can place the word *not* before or after the adjective, but the meaning of the sentence will change.

TIPS ON FORM AND USAGE: Gerunds as subjects

Examples	Explanations
3 • **Being** on time is important. • **Blowing** your nose in public is rude in Japan.	You can use a gerund as the subject of a sentence. Gerunds are often used with an adjective to express an opinion.
4 • **Not** being on time to class is rude. (*It's rude to be late to class.*) • Being on time to class is **not** rude. (*It's okay to be on time to class.*)	You can place the word *not* before or after the gerund, but the meaning of the sentence will be different.

Restate the information in each sentence.

a. It's important to understand the customs in different cultures.
   Understanding the customs in different cultures is important.

b. It's useful to read about a country before you go there.
   Reading about a country before you go there is useful.

c. In some cultures, eating with your fingers is rude.
   It's rude to eat with your fingers in some cultures.

d. In some countries it's important to take your shoes off before you go inside.
   Taking your shoes off before you go inside is important in some countries.

e. Putting your feet up on the furniture is not polite in some cultures.
   It's not polite to put your put up on the furniture in some cultures.

f. In many countries it's rude to hang up the phone without saying good-bye.
   It's rude to hang up the phone without saying good-bye in many countries.

g. Showing someone the bottom of your foot is very impolite in some cultures.
   It's very impolite to show someone the bottom of your foot in some cultures.

h. In many countries it's rude to point at someone with your finger.
   It's rude to point at someone with your finger in many countries.

UNIT 4: Because, (in order) to, for

Answers from page 22

A. Why did women wear very wide skirts?
Because it was the fashion.

B. Why did government officials in China wear long blue robes?
To show their profession.

C. Why did soldiers wear armor?
For protection.

TIPS ON FORM AND USAGE

	Examples	*Explanations*
1	• He put on a sweater **because he was cold.** • Women wore wide skirts **because they wanted to be fashionable.**	Use *because* + a subject and a verb to give a reason.
2	• It's important to wear a hat **to keep** warm. • You should wear sunglasses **to protect** your eyes.	Use *(in order) to* + a verb to state a purpose.
3	• Some people carry umbrellas **for protection** from the sun.	Use *for* + a noun to state a purpose.

---

1. Circle the subject and underline the verb in each *because* clause.

> I wore a suit and tie …
> • because I wanted to look good.
> • because I had an important meeting.

Now complete each sentence in two different ways.

> She wore a T-shirt because …
> • *it was comfortable*
> • *she wanted to keep warm.*

> He took off his coat because …
> • *He was uncomfortable*
> • *He was hot*

2. Choose a verb or a noun to complete each of these sentences.

verbs	nouns
to protect	for protection
to stay warm	for warmth

a. You should wear a heavy coat *to stay warm*.
b. Soldiers wear helmets *for protection*.
c. Some people wear sunglasses *to protect* their eyes from the sun.
d. The Mattisons wear heavy coats *for warmth*.

UNIT 5: Does too/doesn't either; so does/neither does

TIPS ON FORM AND USAGE

Examples	Explanations
① • **Both** my mother **and** my father play the piano. • My mother **and** my father **both** play the piano. (= *My mother plays the piano. My father plays the piano.*)	You can combine two positive statements using *both* … *and* … to describe what two people have in common.
② • **Neither** my mother **nor** my father plays the guitar. (= *My mother doesn't play the guitar. My father doesn't play the guitar.*)	You can combine two negative statements using *neither* … *nor* … to describe what two people have in common.
③ • My sister likes to travel **and so do I.** **and I do too.** • I like to travel **and so does my sister.** **and my sister does too.** (= *My sister likes to travel. I like to travel.*)	You can combine two positive statements using *so do/so does* or *do too/does too.*
④ • My brother doesn't smoke **and neither do I.** **and I don't either.** • I don't smoke **and neither does my brother.** **and my brother doesn't either.** (= *My brother doesn't smoke. I don't smoke.*)	You can combine two negative statements using *neither do/neither does* or *don't either/doesn't either.*
⑤ • My father **is** a teacher and so **am** I. • My father **was** born in China and so **was** I. • My sister **went** to the beach and so **did** I. • My parents **didn't** go to the movies and I **didn't** either.	The verb tenses in the two parts of the sentence match.

1. Find and correct the mistakes in these sentences.
(Some statements may be correct.)

a. I don't like to cook and ~~so my brother.~~ *neither does my brother*

b. My grandparents live in an apartment and my parents too.

c. My brother doesn't eat meat and my sister doesn't neither. *either*

d. I went on vacation last summer and so does my family. *so did*

e. I didn't study French and ~~so didn't~~ my sister. *neither did*

f. My friend likes to watch movies on TV and so do I.

g. I don't like chocolate and my friends don't either.

2. Match the two parts of the sentences below.

a. Manuel was late yesterday — and neither did my wife.

b. They left early — and Roberto was too.

c. I didn't eat dinner — and I don't either.

d. A lot of people don't like cold weather — and so are mine.

e. I get up early every morning — and so did we.

f. Her parents are from Mexico City — and all my friends do too.

UNIT 6: *Comparative adjectives*

Answers from page 34
a. That's false. **b.** That's true. **c.** That's false. **d.** That's true. **e.** That's true.

- **Which comparative adjectives end in *-er*?**
smaller, bigger, harder
- **Which comparative adjectives use the word *more*?**
more difficult, more expensive

TIPS ON FORM AND USAGE

	Examples	*Explanations*
1	sick ⟶ sicker safe ⟶ safer	For most one-syllable adjectives, add *-er* to form the comparative.
2	big ⟶ bigger hot ⟶ hotter sad ⟶ sadder	Some one-syllable adjectives end in a single vowel and consonant. For these adjectives, double the consonant and add *-er*.
3	happy ⟶ happier silly ⟶ sillier	For two-syllable adjectives that end in *-y*, change the *-y* to *-i* and add *-er*.
4	beautiful ⟶ more beautiful useful ⟶ more useful dangerous ⟶ more dangerous	For most adjectives with two or more syllables, use the word *more* + the adjective.
5	good ⟶ better bad ⟶ worse far ⟶ farther	A few adjectives have irregular comparative forms.
6	• Cars are **safer now than** they were **before**. • It's **safer** to fly **than** to drive.	We use comparative adjectives to compare someone or something at different times. We also use comparatives to compare two people or two things. We often use the word *than* after a comparative adjective.
7	• I want to get a **smaller** TV. • Someday I hope to build a **bigger** **house**.	You can use a comparative adjective before a noun.
8	• I feel **a lot** better today. • It's **much** easier to travel nowadays.	We often use an adverb before a comparative adjective.

Use the information in the chart to write the comparative form of these adjectives.

Adjective	Comparative Form	Adjective	Comparative Form
old	older	ugly	uglier
lazy	lazier	expensive	more expensive
thin	thinner	interesting	more interesting

UNIT 7: *Present perfect tense*

Answers from page 42
- **Look at the verbs in each pair of sentences. How are they different?**
The first sentence in each pair has a verb with *has* or *have* + a past participle.
The second sentence in each pair uses the simple past tense.
- **Which sentence in each pair tells about a specific time in the past? What words in each sentence help you to know?**
The second sentence in each pair tells about a specific time in the past. The words *last year, two years ago, when you were a child,* and *in high school* help you to know.

TIPS ON FORM AND USAGE

(1)

		Examples			Explanations

I	You		**have**		To form the present perfect, use
We	They				*have/has* or *have not/has not* +
				played volleyball.	past participle.
He	She	**has**			

Have	I	you			To form a question, place the subject
	we	they			of the verb between *have/has* and the
				ever **ridden** a horse?	past participle.
Has	she	he			

> A list of irregular verbs appears on page 103.

(2)
- I **have tried** a lot of different sports.
- She **has played** basketball a million times.

We use the present perfect to tell about things that happened at an unspecified time <u>before now.</u>

(3)
- **Have** you **ever** seen a barracuda?
- **Has** your teacher **ever** gone skiing?

Ever means *at any time.* You can use *ever* + the present perfect to ask if something happened at any time <u>before now.</u>

(4)
- We **have never been** to a car race.
- My father **has never been** in a boat.

Never means *not at any time.* You can use *never* + the present perfect to show that something has <u>not</u> happened at any time <u>up to now.</u>

---

1. **Complete these sentences using the present perfect.**

   a. Bill Mattison _____ skiing in France several times. (*go*)

   b. The Mattisons _____ a lot of injured skiers. (*help*)

   c. Aaron Chang _____ a lot of photographs of surfers. (*take*)

   d. Julie Krone _____ a lot of horse races. (*win*)

   e. I _____ never _____ a camel. Have you? (*ride*)

   f. _____ you ever _____ an abacus? (*use*)

2. **Choose the correct verb to complete each sentence.**

   a. Last year my brother _____ his bike across Japan. (*has ridden/rode*)

   b. My sister _____ snorkeling several times but I never have. (*has gone/went*)

   c. Gabrielle Reece _____ out of an airplane on her TV show last year. (*has jumped/jumped*)

   d. Mark Allen _____ his first triathlon in 1983. (*has entered/entered*)

UNIT 8: *Superlative adjectives*

Answers from page 48
- **Which adjectives end in** *-est?*
coldest, largest
- **Which adjectives are used with the word** *most?* **Why?**
Beautiful, popular, and *unusual* are used with *most.* These adjectives are longer:
Each has three syllables.

TIPS ON FORM AND USAGE

	Examples	Explanations
1	old ⟶ the oldest clean ⟶ the cleanest	For most one-syllable adjectives, add *-est.*
2	big ⟶ the biggest hot ⟶ the hottest sad ⟶ the saddest	Some adjectives end in a single vowel and consonant. For these adjectives, double the consonant and add *-est.*
3	busy ⟶ the busiest ugly ⟶ the ugliest	For two-syllable adjectives ending in *-y,* change the *-y* to *-i* and add *-est.*
4	wonderful ⟶ the most wonderful interesting ⟶ the most interesting	For most two and three-syllable adjectives, use the word *most* + the adjective.
5	good ⟶ the best bad ⟶ the worst far ⟶ farthest	Some adjectives have irregular forms.
6	• We're going to **the best** restaurant in town. • What's **the largest** city in Mexico?	We use superlative adjectives to show how one person or thing in a group is special.
7	• What's the largest city **in South America?** • What's the largest country **in the world?**	We often use a superlative adjective to identify the group we are talking about.
8	• Tokyo is **one of the cleanest** cities in the world.	We often use superlative adjectives with the expression "one of the ...."

Complete these sentences. Use the superlative form of the adjectives in parentheses.

a. French Guiana is _____ country in South America. *(small)*

b. _____ island south of Australia is Tasmania. *(large)*

c. Greenland is _____ island in the world. *(big)*

d. Many people think that Bali is one of the _____ places on Earth. *(beautiful)*

e. Canada has _____ coastline of any country in the world. *(long)*

f. Heathrow is _____ airport in Europe. *(busy)*

g. Tokyo is one of _____ places to live in the world. *(expensive)*

UNIT 9: *Count/Noncount nouns*

Answers from page 54
- Which nouns can you use with *a* or *an*?
count nouns
- Which nouns have a plural form?
count nouns
- Which nouns do you always use with a singular verb?
noncount nouns

TIPS ON FORM AND USAGE: *Count/Noncount nouns*

Examples	Explanations
1 • This **picture is** beautiful. • These **pictures are** wonderful. • **Jewelry is** an expensive gift. • **Money is** not always an appropriate gift.	Count nouns can be singular or plural. Noncount nouns are always singular.
2 • One of my friends gave me **a** great book. • I don't need **an** answering machine. • I don't need money. • I love fruit.	You can use *a* or *an* with singular count nouns. We don't use *a* or *an* with noncount nouns.
3 • She gave me **some** beautiful flowers. • He gave me **some** beautiful jewelry. • I really don't need **any** flowers. • You shouldn't give him **any** money.	We often use *some* or *any* with count nouns and noncount nouns.
4 • There is **a box of candy** on the table. • There is **a basket of fruit** on the table. • There is **a bottle of wine** on the table.	We often use noncount nouns with expressions such as *a box of* or *a basket of*, as in *a box of candy* or *a basket of fruit*.

1. **Read these sentences and label the underlined words.**
   Write C (Count noun) or NC (Noncount noun).

   a. I really need a new <u>computer</u>.   *C*
   b. Where are the <u>flowers</u> you bought?   _____
   c. Do you take <u>cream</u> in your coffee?   _____
   d. I bought some jazz <u>CDs</u> last week.   _____
   e. Is it okay to give <u>money</u> as a gift?   _____
   f. I gave my sister some <u>clothes</u> for her birthday.   _____
   g. My sister's boyfriend gave her a <u>box of candy</u>.   _____
   h. Have you ever given anyone a <u>bottle of wine</u>?   _____

UNIT 10: *Relative clauses*

TIPS ON FORM AND USAGE

Examples	*Explanations*
(1) • I have a friend **who loves horror movies.** (= *I have a friend. My friend loves horror movies.*) • There's a movie theater in town **that only shows old movies.** (= *There's a movie theater in town. It only shows old movies.*)	A relative clause describes or gives more information about a person or thing.
(2) • I have **a friend who** loves horror movies. • I have **a friend that** loves horror movies. • A blockbuster is **a movie that** is very successful.	You can begin a relative clause with *who* or *that* when you are talking about a <u>person</u>. You can begin a relative clause with *that* when talking about a <u>thing</u>.
(3) • I have **a friend** who **was** in a movie. • I have **two friends** who **were** in a movie.	In the first sentence, the relative clause gives information about one friend. That's why the verb is singular. In the second sentence, the relative clause gives information about two friends. That's why the verb is plural.
(4) • I have a friend **who acted** in a movie. • I saw the movie **that** you **recommended.**	*That* or *who* can be the subject or object of the verb in the relative clause.
(5) • **Do you know the name of the actress who** played Princess Leia in *Star Wars*? • **What do you call the person who** writes the music for a movie? • **What do you call a movie that** has singing and dancing?	We often use relative clauses when we need to ask for a specific word or name.

Circle the words that can correctly complete each question.
(More than one answer may be possible.)

a. Did you see the movie _____ the Cannes Film Festival last year?

      who won   that won   that win

b. Do you know the name of the actor _____ in *Eat, Drink, Man, Woman*?

      who starred   that starred   that star

c. Do you know the name of the famous movie director _____ *The Seven Samurai*?

      who make   that made   who makes

d. What do you call the people _____ about movies in the newspaper?

      who writes   that writes   who write

UNIT 11: If *clauses with modals*

a. you will get a lot of zinc; you might improve your memory **b.** they won't stay that way **c.** you might damage your hearing

• **What verb tense is used in the *if* clauses?**

the simple present

• **When do you use the word *might* in the main clause? When do you use *will*?**

Use *might* to show a possible consequence. Use *will* to show a definite consequence.

TIPS ON FORM AND USAGE

Examples	*Explanations*
1 • If you drink a lot of coffee, **you might feel shaky later.** • If you get sick, **you won't be able to work tomorrow.** • If you take your medicine, **you will feel better.** • If he works too hard, **he might get sick.**	These sentences tell what *might* or *will* happen in the future under certain circumstances. Use the simple present in the *if* clause and *will* or *might* + verb in the main clause.
2 • If you stay up all night, you **will** be sleepy tomorrow. (It's certain.) • If you smoke, you **might** get cancer someday. (It's possible.)	Use *will* to describe a definite future consequence. Use *might* to describe a possible future consequence.
3 • You won't get better **if you don't go to the doctor.** • **If you don't go to the doctor,** you won't get better.	The *if* clause can go before or after the main clause.
4 • If you **don't** smoke, you will feel better. • If you eat too much candy, you **won't** feel very well. • If you **don't** take your medicine, you **won't** feel better.	You can use negatives in both clauses.

Complete each sentence with a form of the verb in parentheses.

a. If you _____ yourself, you might get sick. (*take care of*)

b. If you take this medicine, you _____ better. (*feel*)

c. You might have more energy if you _____ some exercise. (*get*)

d. If you _____ vitamins, you might not get sick. (*take*)

e. You _____ sleepy tomorrow if you don't get enough sleep tonight. (*be*)

UNIT 12: Be going to; *present continuous*

Answers from page 74
- What verb tenses can you use to identify a future plan?
  future with be going to, *the simple present continuous*

TIPS ON FORM AND USAGE

Examples	*Explanations*
1 • **I'm going** to see the new Sylvester Stallone movie tonight. • **I'm meeting** my friends at 7:00 in front of the theater.	You can use both *be going to* and the present continuous (*be* + the *-ing* form of the verb) to talk about future plans.
2 • **We're going to** get a new car soon. • **I'm going to** stay up late tonight. • **She's going to** continue studying English. • What **are** you **going to** do?	We often use *be going to* to talk about future plans, especially when we want to emphasize a <u>future decision</u>.
3 • I'm going to go home after class today. • I'm going home after class today. • We're going to go out tonight. • We're going out tonight.	We sometimes shorten *going to go* to *going*.
4 • **We're getting** a new car next week. • What **are** we **having** for dinner tonight? • **We're having** fish for dinner tonight.	We often use the present continuous to talk about future plans and intentions, especially when we want to emphasize a <u>future arrangement</u> in which the time and place have been decided.

Answer the questions below.

a. What are you going to do after class today?

_____

b. Are you going on vacation soon?

_____

c. What are you having for dinner tonight?

_____

d. What are you planning to do after dinner?

_____

e. What are you going to do tomorrow?

_____

f. Are you going to continue studying English next year?

_____

Irregular Verbs

BASE FORM	SIMPLE PAST	PAST PARTICIPLE
be	was/were	been
become	became	become
begin	began	begun
build	built	built
buy	bought	bought
catch	caught	caught
choose	chose	chosen
come	came	come
cost	cost	cost
do	did	done
drink	drank	drunk
drive	drove	driven
eat	ate	eaten
fall	fell	fallen
feel	felt	felt
find	found	found
fly	flew	flown
get	got	gotten
give	gave	given
go	went	gone
grow	grew	grown
hang (out)	hung (out)	hung (out)
have	had	had
hear	heard	heard
hold	held	held
keep	kept	kept
know	knew	known
lead	led	led
leave	left	left
lose	lost	lost
make	made	made
meet	met	met
put	put	put
read /rid/	read /rɛd/	read /rɛd/
ride	rode	ridden
run	ran	run
say	said	said
see	saw	seen
seek	sought	sought
send	sent	sent
set (out)	set (out)	set (out)
shake	shook	shaken
show	showed	showed/shown
sit	sat	sat
sleep	slept	slept
speak	spoke	spoken
spend	spent	spent
swim	swam	swum
take (off)	took (off)	taken (off)
tell	told	told
think	thought	thought
understand	understood	understood
wake (up)	woke (up)	woken (up)
wear	wore	worn
win	won	won
wind	wound	wound
write	wrote	written